ELEMENTS OF ISLAMIC STUDIES

by
Maulana Syed Saeed Akhtar Rizvi

Published in the
Small Book Series by
PYAM-E-AMAN
P.O. BOX 390
BLOOMFIELD, NJ 07003
U.S.A.

Distributors:
TAHRIKE TARSILE QUR'AN, INC.
Publishers and Distributors of Holy Qur'an
P.O. Box 1115
Elmhurst, New York 11373

First Revised U.S. Edition 1989

Library of Congress Catalog Number: 89-051359
British Library Cataloguing in Publication Data
ISBN: 0-940368-99-4

Typeset By
Yasmin Jaffer & Abbas Rahim

Distributors in England:
Murtaza Bandali/ALIF International
37 Princes Ave.
Watford, Herts WD1 7RR
England, U.K.

Distributors in Canada:
MIHRAB Publishers & Book Distributors Canada
36 Robbinstone Drive
Scarborough, Ontario
Canada, M1B 2E6

INTRODUCTION

This book, written by Allama S. Saeed Akhtar Rizvi, was first published in 1968 in Africa by Haji Muhammad A. Khimji.

It captured our imagination, for it was this type of book we had been searching for our children. It contains the most fundamental aspects of our religion which they should know before their minds are covered with the dust of Western ideas. Originally written for African children, it was revised again and again and was adapted for use by the American Muslims, keeping in view that its usefulness should not diminish in any way.

The beauty of the first American edition was that it was a combined undertaking of all the Jaffery associations of metropolitan New York and New Jersey.

This issue in your hand, has been completely revised and has been thoroughly reviewed although there has been no major change. Even the sequence is the same as before; however, for a thorough reader or critic, lot of changes will be easily noticeable. And all this revision has added to the usefulness of this valuable book.

We are highly indebted to the Bilal Mission of Tanzania for their permission to us to reprint this book. We also sincerely thank all those friends who helped us in previous editions of this book. However, our special thanks are due to Maulana Syed Tilmiz Hasnain Rizvi, Director, Islamic Central Directorate, Englewood, N.J. for his thorough and exhaustive review of the entire book.

Thanks are also due to the members of our community who received this book so enthusiastically. May Allah bless all of them - His servants.

We would not have been able to fulfill our duties if we forgot to thank Almighty Allah Who gave us perseverence and patience throughout the period. But for His guidance and help, the job could not have been completed. We fervently hope He accepts our small service.

DR. SYED MANZOOR NAQI RIZVI
for PYAM-E-AMAN
P.O. BOX 390,
BLOOMFIELD, N.J. 07003

i

CONTENTS

iii

LESSON 1

KALEMA
LA ILAAHA IL-LAL-LAH
MUHAMMAD-UR-RASOOLULLAH
ALI'YUN WALI'YULLAH
WA WASI-YO-RASOO'LILLAH

WA KHALIFA-TOHU BILA FASL

Its Meaning
There is no god but Allah
Muhammad is Allah's Messenger
Ali is Wali (friend) of Allah
and he is the successor of the
Prophet;
and he is the First Khalifa of the
Prophet (S.A.W.)

LESSON 2

The Names of the PANJATAN - the Five Holy Ones:

1. Hadret Muhammad Mustafa (S.A.W.)

2. Hadret Ali ibn-e-Abi Talib (A.S.)

3. Hadret Sayedda Fatima Zahra (S.A.)

4. Hadret Imam Hasan (A.S.)

5. Hadret Imam Husain (A.S.).

LESSON 3

Our Prophet, Hadret Muhammad Mustafa (S.A.W.); his daughter, Hadret Sayedda Fatima Zahra (S.A.), and the 12 Aimma (A.S.), form the group of the Fourteen Masoomeen. All of them are Ma'asoom (infallible, sinless).

THE FOURTEEN MASOOMEEN

1. Abul Qasim Muhammad ibn-e-Abdullah Al-Mustafa (S.A.W.)
   53 B.H. - 11 A.H.

2. Ummus Sibtain Hadret Fatima bint-e-Muhammad Az-Zahra (A.S.)
   8 B.H. - 11 A.H.

1

3. Abul-Hasan Ali ibn-e-Abi Talib Al-Murtada, son of Abu Talib, and first cousin of our Prophet, Muhammad; married to Hadret Fatima Zahra, the daughter of our Prophet. 23 B.H. - 40 A.H.

4. Abu Muhammad Hasan ibn-e-Ali, Al-Mujtaba, the elder son of Ali ibn-e-Abi Talib and Fatima Zahra. 3 A.H. - 50 A.H.

5. Abu Abdillah Husain ibn-e-Ali, Sayed-ush-Shuhada, the younger son of Ali ibn-e-Abi Talib and Fatima Zahra. 4 A.H. - 61 A.H.

6. Abu Muhammad Ali ibn-il-Husain, Zayn-ul-Abidin. 38 A.H. - 95 A.H.

7. Abu Jafar Muhammad ibn-e-Ali, Al-Baqir, 57 A.H. - 114 A.H.

8. Abu Abdillah Jafar ibn-e-Muhammad, As-Sadiq, 83 A.H. - 148 A.H.

9. Abu Ibrahim Musa ibn-e-Jafar, Al-Kazim, 128 A.H. - 183 A.H.

10. Abul-Hasan Ali ibn-e-Musa, Ar-Rida, 148 A.H. - 203 A.H.

11. Abu Jafar Muhammad ibn-e-Ali, Al-Jawwad (At-Taqi). 195 A.H. - 220 A.H.

12. Abul-Hasan Ali ibn-e-Muhammad, Al-Hadi (An-Naqi). 213 A.H. - 254 A.H.

13. Abu Muhammad Hasan ibn-e-Ali, Al-Askari, 232 A.H. - 260 A.H.

14. Abul-Qasim Muhammad ibn-e-Hasan, Al-Mahdi, born on 15th of Shaaban, 256 A.H.

The 12th Imam, Muhammad ibn-e-Hasan, Al-Mahdi, is alive till this day but is hidden (as ordained by Allah), and will reappear at a time chosen by Allah. He is the Awaited one, and Mahdi, who will revive Islam and will spread it throughout the world.

Whenever we utter or hear the name of our Prophet (S.A.W.), we should recite Salawat and we should say, SALLALLAHO ALAYHI WA AALIHI WA SALLAM (Peace of Allah be on him and his progeny). Whenever we utter or hear the names of other Masoomeen, we should say

2

ALAYHIS-SALAAM. Similarly, we should stand up, as a mark of reverence, whenever we utter or hear the name of the Imam of our time, Imam Mahdi A.S., the twelfth and the last Imam.

LESSON 4
SALAWAT

LAHUMMA SALLAY ALA MUHAMMADIN WA AALE MUHAMMAD.

MEANING OF SALAWAT.
O Allah! Send Thy Blessings to our Prophet Muhammad and his Ahlul-Bayt (Members of his family).

LESSON 5
NAMES OF ULUL-AZM PROPHETS (A.S.):

(There were 5 Ulul-Azm Prophets who brought new shari'ats):
1. Hadret Nuh (A.S.) .... (NOAH)
2. Hadret Ibrahim (A.S.) .... (ABRAHAM)
3. Hadret Musa (A.S.) .... (MOSES)
4. Hadret Isa (A.S.) .... (JESUS)
5. Hadret Muhammad Mustafa (S.A.W.)

LESSON 6
NAMES OF REVEALED BOOKS (ASMANI KUTUB)

Many books were revealed (sent) to the Prophets. Four of them are important. They are 1. Tawrat; 2. Zabur; 3. Injeel; and 4. Qur'an.
You should know that:
1. Tawrat was revealed to Hadret Musa (A.S.).
2. Zabur was revealed to Hadret Dawood (A.S.).
3. Injeel was revealed to Hadret Isa (A.S.).
4. The QUR'AN was revealed to our Holy Prophet Hadret Muhammad Mustafa (S.A.W.).

3

All previous books were cancelled by Allah when the Qur'an was sent. Now it is the only authentic and true book which has to be followed by mankind.

LESSON 7
NAMES OF ISLAMIC MONTHS

1. Muharram; 2. Safar; 3. Rabiul-Awwal; 4.Rabiul-A'kher; 5. Jumadal-Ula; 6. Jumadal-Ukhra; 7. Rajab; 8. Shaban; 9. Ramadan; 10. Shawwal; 11.Zilqada; 12. Zilhijja.

LESSON 8
THE TEACHINGS OF ISLAM

A: THE ROOTS OF RELIGION (USOOL-E-DEEN).

USOOL (Roots): The Fundamental Principles, the beliefs which are essential for a Muslim. These are:

1. TAWHEED (Oneness of God).
2. 'ADL (Justice of God).
3. NUBUWWAT (Prophethood).
4. IMAMAT (Vicegerency of the Prophet).
5. QIYAMAT (Resurrection).

B: THE BRANCHES (FUROO-E-DEEN).

FUROO or branches which call for certain actions: These are:
1. SALAT (Prayer).
2. SOM (Fasting).
3. HAJJ (Pilgrimage).
4. ZAKAT (Wealth Tax).
5. KHUMS (One-fifth Levy).
6. JEHAD (Holy War).
7. AMR BIL MAAROOF (Enjoining the good).
8. NAHIY ANIL MUNKAR (Forbidding the evil).
9. TAWALLA (To love Allah and the 14 Masoomeen).
10. TABARRA (To remain aloof from the enemies of Allah and the 14 Maoomeen).

4

LESSON 9
THE ROOTS OF RELIGION (I)

I. TAWHEED (Oneness of God)

TAWHEED means that ALLAH IS ONE. He has neither any colleague nor any partner. He is neither born of any parent nor has He any wife, children or relatives.

II. 'ADL (Justice of God)

It means that ALLAH is Just. He is not a tyrant. Everybody's awards will depend upon his deeds. He who obeys His (ALLAH's) commands will be awarded a place in Paradise and he who disobeys Him will be sent to Hell.

In this connection Quran says:

ALLAH affirms that there is no god but He; and so do the angels, and those endued with knowledge, He is standing firm in justice. (3:18).

LESSON 10
SIFAT-E-SUBUTIYYAH

In order to understand Tawheed clearly, the attributes of Allah have been grouped as positive and negative.

The positive attributes which are befitting Allah are called Sifat-e-Subutiyyah. They are many in number, but eight of them are usually listed. They are:

1. QADEEM. This means that Allah is Eternal i.e. He has neither a beginning nor an end.
2. QAADIR. It means that Allah is Omnipotent, i.e. He has power over everything, and every affair.
3. AALIM. It means that Allah is Omniscient i.e. He knows everything. Nothing ever remains a secret from Him.
4. HAI. It means that Allah is alive and will remain alive forever.
5. MUREED. This means that Allah has His own discretion in all affairs. He does not do anything under compulsion.
6. MUDRIK. It means that He is All-Perceiving, as-Sami (All Hearing), Baseer (All Seeing), Haadir (Omnipresent). Allah sees and hears everything though He has neither eyes nor ears.

5

7. MUTAKALLIM. It means that Allah is the Master of the word, i.e. He can create speech in anything as He did in a tree for Hadret Musa (A.S.) and in the "Curtain of Light" for Holy Prophet (S.A.W.).

8. SADIQ. This means that Allah is true in His words and promises.

It is impossible to fix any limits to Allah's attributes. This list is not exhaustive, but is essential to understand the Glory of Allah. The attributes are not acquired but are inherent in the conception of Divine Unity.

LESSON 11
SIFAT-E-SALBIYYAH

The Negative Attributes which cannot be found in Allah because they are below His dignity, are called "Sifat-e-Salbiyya." They are many, but like "Sifat-e-Subutiyyah," only eight are listed generally. They are:

1. SHAREEK. The word "Shareek" means a colleague or a partner. Allah has neither a colleague nor a partner.

2. MURAKKAB. This word means "Compound" or "Mixed." Allah is neither made, nor composed, of any material. He cannot be divided even in imagination.

3. MAKAAN. It means "Place." Allah is not confined to any place for He has no JISM (body).

4. HULOOL. It means "entering." Nothing enters Allah nor does He enter anything or anybody. Therefore, the belief of Incarnation in any form is abhorrent to the concept of Divinity.

5. MAHALLE HAWADITH. This means "subject to changes." Allah cannot change.

6. MAR-EE. It means visible. Allah is not visible. He has not been seen, is not seen, and will never be seen, because He does not have a body.

7. IHTIYAJ. It means "dependence" or "need." Allah is not deficient, so he does not need anything.

8. SIFATE ZAYED. This means "added qualifications." The attributes of Allah are not separate from His Being.

For example, when we say that Allah is Aalim, it does not mean that His knowledge is something separate from His existence. In fact, there has never been a time when He was less Aalim and then acquired more

6

knowledge. His Knowledge, His Mercy, His Justice and all His virtues and attributes are His Own Being.

It will thus be seen that according to Islam, ALLAH is the name of God as perceived in the light of the above Positive and Negative Attributes. In other words, Allah is the Creator of the Universe, Self-Existent, the Source of all perfection and free from all defects.

LESSON 12
THE ROOTS OF RELIGION (II)
III. NUBUWWAT (Prophethood)

The conception of Prophethood follows from the premises that it is the Will of ALLAH that every human being should pursue a defined code of life and follow certain principles of conduct. ALLAH therefore had to send messengers (prophets A.S.) to acquaint mankind with these principles and the code of life.

1B - THE KAABA 'The House of Allah.'
1A - MECCA HOLY MOSQUE (Mecca).

7

Quran says:
Nor would We punish without sending Messengers to give warning.
(17:15)
The third Usool - NUBUWWAT - calls for belief in all the prophets (A.S.) sent by Allah from time to time for the guidance of humanity. According to Islam, Allah sent 124,000 prophets in all. Adam (A.S.) was the first of them. Nuh (A.S.) (Noah), Ibrahim (A.S.) (Abraham), Musa (A.S.) (Moses) and Isa (A.S.) (Jesus) were other prominent prophets (peace be on them all). Our Prophet, Hadret Muhammad Mustafa (S.A.W.), was the last. Some prophets came with new Shari'ats (codes of life) while others followed and spread the Shari'ats of their forerunners.

Since the words of a prophet are to be obeyed and his actions are to serve as a guide, it follows that every prophet should be infallible in his thoughts, words and deeds.

According to Islam the entire universe came into existence through the Will of the Creator and was created with a definite purpose. Says the Holy Quran:

Verily! In the creation of the Heavens and the Earth and in the variation of the night and the day are signs for the men of understanding who standing and sitting and reclining celebrate the praise of Allah and ponder on the creation of the Heavens and Earth, "O our Lord!" they say, "Thou hast not created this in vain." (3:190,191)

And further the specific purpose of creation is:
'I have not created the jinn and the human beings but to obey Me.' 51:56
Now, to explain this "Divine Will" came the "Divine Messengers" known as the prophets.
Verily! Allah hath chosen Adam (A.S.) and Noah (A.S.), the progeny of Abraham (A.S.) and the progeny of Imran above the worlds, the descendants one of the other. Allah is One Who hears and knows. 2:33-34
The prophets (A.S.) never disagreed in fundamentals. Generally, the prophets (A.S.) were deputed for specified communities, regions or periods. Muhammad (S.A.W.), the Last of the Divine Messengers, was sent to express the Will of ALLAH for the entire humanity, and for all times to come.

To quote Quran:
We have not sent thee but as a MERCY unto all the worlds. 21:107
And We have not sent thee but as a universal messenger to announce and to warn. But most of the people do not understand. (34:28)

8

Say unto them: O men! I am ALLAH'S Messenger to YOU ALL: Whose is the Kingdom of the Heavens and the Earth! There is no god but He! He maketh alive and killeth! Therefore believe in ALLAH, and His Messenger, the Makkan Prophet-who believeth in ALLAH and His word; and follow him that ye may be guided right. 7:158

Islam is a perfect code of life for the entire humanity without distinction of classes and countries. It lays great emphasis on the purification of the 'self' of an individual based on the fundamental principles - belief in Oneness of ALLAH and in the Life Hereafter. This will, ultimately, lead to universal brotherhood and a peaceful world.

LESSON 13
THE ROOTS OF RELIGION (III)
IV. IMAMAT [Vicegerency of the Prophet (S.A.W.)]

During his lifetime, Prophet Muhammad (S.A.W.) had announced on several occasions that the responsibility for the guidance of the Muslim community would rest, after him, on certain named persons as ordained by ALLAH. These persons are known as Imams A.S., (Vicegerents of the Prophet S.A.W.). The Imam is the deputy of the Prophet, in every respect. Like the Prophet, (S.A.W.), therefore, the Imam should also be infallible in his thoughts, words and deeds.

You have already been taught the names of those Imams (A.S.) in Lesson 3.

There are clear references in the Holy Quran about belief in the Imams A.S. as for example:

O you who believe! Obey ALLAH and obey the Messenger and those among you invested with Divine Authority; and if ye differ, bring it before ALLAH and the Messenger if ye believe in ALLAH and the Last Day. This is the best and the fairest way of settlement. (4:59)

(And remember) The Day (of Judgment) when We shall call all human beings with their Imams. 17:71

Referring to Imams A.S., the Prophet S.A.W. has further emphasized:

One who dies and does not recognize the Imam (A.S.) of his time, dies the death of a pagan.

On the Day of Resurrection, every nation will be summoned along with the IMAM A.S. of its time.

9

V. QIYAMAT (Resurrection)

There is a life Hereafter. After death, an individual gets the reward or the punishment for the deeds he has performed before death. For this purpose, on a certain day called the "Day of Judgment," all the dead would be resurrected from their graves and awarded Heaven or Hell, depending on the merits of their actions in this world.

The Quran says:

Beware when the Event (Qiyamat) would occur
No soul would then falsify its occurrence,
(Many) will it bring low,
(Many) will it bring high;
When the earth would be shaken to its depths,
And the mountains would crumble
becoming dust scattered all about. 56:1-6

The day of Qiyamat will be thousands of years in duration as has been written in the Holy Quran. The sun on that day will come down very low and the earth will be red-hot like heated copper.

LESSON 14
THE BRANCHES OF RELIGION (I)
FUROO-E-DEEN

Furoo-e-Deen means the Branches of Religion. It has many branches but usually six to ten are taught to the children. They are explained below.

I. PRAYER

The daily five prayers and other five prayers which are detailed elsewhere are all obligatory and should be performed at proper times in fulfillment of prescribed conditions.

The prayers are obligatory on adults (Baligh). For the purpose of fulfilling religious obligations, a boy is deemed to be an adult on completion of his fifteenth year, and a girl on completion of her ninth year.

The Quran has repeatedly enjoined upon every Muslim the offering of prayers (Iqamat-e-Salat):

Verily! I am ALLAH; there is no god but I, therefore, submit to Me and offer prayers to celebrate My praise. 20:14.

Recite from the Book revealed to thee and offer prayer! Prayer restrains from filth and evil without doubt, and ALLAH knows what you do. 29:45 (Luqman said) O my son! Offer prayer and enjoin the good and forbid the evil and be patient whatever betide thee for this is firmness in the conduct of affairs. 31:17

II. SOM (Fasting)

Fasting is obligatory for every Muslim adult, male or female, for the entire lunar month of Ramadan every year. The fast lasts just from the true dawn till the commencement of night. During the fast, one has to abstain from eating, drinking, smoking and some other actions. In this regard, the Quran says:

O ye who believe! Fasting is prescribed to you, as it was prescribed to those before you, that ye may acquire piety.

So every one of you who is present (at his home) during this month, should spend it in fasting. (2:185)

LESSON 15
THE BRANCHES OF RELIGION (II)
III. HAJJ (Pilgrimage)

Every Mulsim is enjoined to go to Makkah, once in the lifetime, for pilgrimage which becomes obligatory when a man has funds enough for his return journey as well as maintenance of his family, and is able to fulfill other conditions laid down for Hajj. This is performed on the 9th day of the last month of the Islamic (Lunar) calender - Dhil'hijja. (Zilhajj).

Qur'an says: Proclaim the Hajj among people so that they come to you on foot and on camels of any kind from deep and distant places. 22:27.

The Hajj of the House of ALLAH (Ka'ba) is obligatory on every one who has means for the journey to it.

IV. ZAKAT (Wealth Tax)

It is incumbent upon everyone to pay wealth tax on gold, silver, cattle and agricultural produce, when all conditions are fulfilled. This contribution is termed ZAKAT and should be paid to deserving poor (Shia Ithna Ashri) believers.

The Quran has commanded the payment of "Zakat" almost as emphatically as the saying of prayers so much so that almost every verse which speaks of prayers, speaks of payment of Zakat, e.g.:

And offer prayers.
And pay Zakat.
And bow down with those
Who bow down (in worship). 2:43

V. KHUMS (One-Fifth Levy on Savings)

Setting aside one-fifth of the amount of a year's savings, (after deducting all the lawful expenses from the earnings of that year) is called KHUMS.

Sadaat [descendents of the Holy Prophet (S.A.W.)] provided they are Ithnaasheri and poor, will get half of the Khums, while the other half belongs to the Imam (A.S.) which during his Ghaybat (occultation) must be handed over to a Mujtahid, (Naib-e-Imam).

The Quranic command for this is as follows:

And know that out of all wealth that you may acquire, one-fifth of it is for ALLAH, and for the Messenger and for his kinsmen, and the orphans, the poor and the wayfarer. (8:41)

LESSON 16
THE BRANCHES OF RELIGION (III)
VI. JEHAD (The Holy War)

Defense is unquestionably one of the most important duties of a community. Islam provides for the defense of the Muslim community by the imposition of what is called JEHAD. It means fighting in the path of Allah in response to the call from the Prophet (S.A.W) or the Imam (A.S.) of the Age.

And fight in the cause of ALLAH against those who fight against you: but do not transgress bacause ALLAH does not love transgressors. (2:190)

VII. AMR BIL MAAROOF

It means enjoining the good. If a person does not fulfill the obligations laid down by Allah, it is obligatory on us to guide him to the right path provided we have a hope that he will follow our guidance.

12

VIII. NAHIY ANIL MUNKAR

It means forbidding the prohibited things or works. We should ask any man found doing things prohibited by Allah to refrain from such deeds, provided we have a hope that he will act on our advice.

IX. TAWALLA

It means to love Allah and the fourteen Masoomeen and be friendly with their followers.

X. TABARRA

It means that we should stay away from the enemies of Allah and the fourteen Masoomeen.

THE GREEN DOME. The Mosque of Prophets (S.A.W.).

13

IJTIHAD AND TAQLEED

In every sphere of life we have to listen to the advice of the experts in that field. Likewise, in the matter of Islamic Laws, we must obey the rulings of the experts of the Law. Those experts are called Mujtahids, and the act of obeying their rulings is called Taqleed.

Following are the conditions necessary in a Merja'e-Taqleed:
1. He must be an adult (baligh)
2. He must be wise ('aqil)
3. He must have Faith (Iman)
4. He must be a male
5. He must be a Mujtahid (he must be qualified by knowledge and experience to exercise Ijtihad).
6. He must be Just (he must have a sense of 'adl i.e. Justice)
7. He must be a legitimate child of his parents
8. He must have a good memory
9. He must be alive at the time of beginning the Taqleed.

Note: A Merja'e-taqleed must be more knowledgeable than other Mujtahideen. He is called an Aalam.

LESSON 17
USEFUL EXPLANATIONS
PART 1

1. WAJIB - obligatory, necessary, incumbent, mandatory - an act which must be performed. You will be rewarded for performing it and punished for neglecting it, e.g., the daily prayers, the fasting of Ramadan.
2. EHTIYAT-E-WAJIB - precautionarily obligatory. Its significance is the same as that of wajib with the difference that in the problems where a mujtahid says it is "precautionarily obligatory," one has the option of leaving his taqleed (following) in this particular problem, and following the ruling of the second-best mujtahid in that problem.
3. HARAM - forbidden, prohibited. It is necessary to abstain from the acts which are haram. If someone performs a haram act, he will be punished, e.g., eating pork.
4. SUNNAT, MUSTAHAB - recommended, desirable. The acts whose neglect is not punished, but whose performance is rewarded, e.g., the call for prayers (adhan).

14

5. MAKROOH - reprehensible, disliked. The acts whose performance is not punished, but whose avoidance is rewarded, e.g., eating in the state of janabat.

6. JA'IZ, HALAL, MUBAH - permitted, lawful, allowed. The acts or the things which are permitted and lawful. There is no reward for performing it and no punishment for neglecting it, e.g., drinking tea.

PART II

1. MUSLIM: One who believes in Allah, His Prophet S.A.W. and the Day of Resurrection (Qiyamat), recites Kalema and accepts the commands of Allah and His Prophet S.A.W. as true, is called a Muslim.

2. MOMIN: A Muslim who believes that Allah is Adil (just) and the twelve Imams (mentioned in Lesson 3) are the only rightful successors of the Holy Prophet (S.A.W.) and that all of them were appointed by Allah, is called a Momin.

3. KAFIR: He who does not believe in God or His Prophet S.A.W. or in Qiyamat is a KAFIR (Unbeliever).

4. MUSHRIK: One who believes that Allah has one or more colleagues or partners is called a MUSHRIK.

5. MUNAFIQ: One who proclaims his belief in Allah and his Prophet (A.S.) and also recites the Kalema but does not have faith in them at heart, and is inimical toward them inwardly, is called a MUNAFIQ-in plain terms, a hypocrite.

LESSON 18
USEFUL EXPLANATIONS
PART III

1. GHASBI: Anything taken from others without their consent; likewise, anything taken from others in normal transaction with the intention of not paying its price, or returning it.

2. MUBAH: Legal; lawful; taken with consent of the owner.

3. HADATH: Those Najasats which require Niyyat (intention) for cleaning like those things after which Wudu (Wuzu) or Ghusl becomes necessary. Hadath is of two kinds: Big and Small.

4. HADATH-E-AKBER (Big): Those things which require Ghusl for being clean, like Janabat, Haid (Haiz), Nifas, Istihada (Istihaza) and Mass-e-Mayyit.

15

5. HADATH-E-ASGHER (Small): Those things which require Wudu (Wuzu) for being clean, like sleep, etc.

6. KHABATH: Those Najasats which do not require Niyyat for cleaning like all the Najasats described in Lesson 19.

7. MUWALAT: To do any work, e.g., Wudu (Wuzu) without interruption; to perform all parts of a work one after another without interval.

8. TARTIB: To perform every work in the same order which has been approved by the Shariat.

NOTE: The difference between Hadath and Khabath may be described thus: Khabath is external Najasat and therefore there is no need of Niyyat for cleaning it; while Hadath is not an external but spiritual uncleanliness, and therefore it requires the attention and intention of spirit to clean it.

NOTE 2: To make the above point more clear, it is advisable to mention that, for example, when a person goes to W.C, he acquires both kinds of Najasat, i.e. the Khabath and Hadath,

Khabath is the external Najasat which he cleanses there without any Niyyat, and thus his body becomes Tahir. But still, he cannot pray because the spiritual Najasat i.e., Hadath has not been removed. It will be removed when he will perform Wudu (with Niyyat) and then he will be qualified spiritually to converse with Allah.

LESSON 19
NAJASAT

Najasat (plural Najasaat) means a thing which is unclean in itself, and makes other things unclean by contact. There are ten (10) Najasaat: 1. and 2. Urine and stool of those living things whose meat is Haram, (not allowed to be eaten) and whose blood comes out with a gush, when slaughtered, other than birds. For example, the urine of sheep is not Najis, because its meat is not Haram though its blood comes out with a gush. Likewise, the stool of snake is not Najis because its blood does not come out with a gush, though its meat is Haram.

NOTE: Urine and Stool of those animals are Najis which eat refuse of human beings or have drunk milk of pig.

3. and 4. Blood and semen of those living things whose blood comes out with a gush, whether they be Halal or Haram. So these two things of human beings are Najis.

5. Dead body of those living things whose blood comes out with a gush. But there are some exceptions: those parts which have no life in them

during lifetime; like hair, nail, bone, teeth, etc., are not Najis. The corpse of a Muslim is Najis after being cold and before being washed. Before being cold it is Tahir; after being washed, it is Tahir. The limbs which are cut from a living body (as in operation) are treated as corpse. (Ivory is taken out from dead elephant; still it is not Najis, because it is a part which has no life in the lifetime of the elephant. You may think other examples yourself).

6. The dog.
7. The pig.
8. Kafir.
9. The Liquor (liquid intoxicant).
10. Fuqqa (mild beer).

NOTE: The sweat that comes out during or after becoming unlawfully 'Junub' and the sweat of the animal which eats refuse of human beings are not Najis; but prayer with such sweat on body or clothes is not allowed.

LESSON 20
MUTAHHIRAT (I)

Mutahhirat i.e. the things which make a najis thing clean. These are 12 as follows:
1. Water
2. Earth
3. Sun
4. Istihala
5. Inqilab
6. Intiqal
7. Islam
8. Tabaiat
9. Zawal-e-Ain-e-Najasat
10. Istibra of Najasat-eating animals
11. Ghaibat-e-Muslim
12. Flowing of blood in normal quantity from a lawfully slaughtered animal.

NOTE: Mutahhirat are 12 according to the Fatwa of Ayetullah Abul Qasim Al-Khoi.

1. WATER:
(a) Depending on purity or impurity, water is of two kinds: Mutlaq i.e., pure water; and Mudaf (Muzaf) i.e., mixed water. Mixed water cannot

17

make anything clean. Instead, it itself becomes unclean by coming into contact with anything unclean.

(b) Pure water is of 5 kinds: (1) Rain water; (2) Running water; (3) Well water; (4) Still water about a Kur or more than a Kur; (5) Still water less than a Kur.

Water cleanses a Najis thing on the condition that the water is (1) Mutlaq, (2) clean (Tahir), and (3) does not become Mudaf (Muzaf) by coming into contact with that Najasat, and (4) all the Najasat is washed away from that Najis thing.

Rain water, running water (like sea, river, stream, spring, etc.) and well water make things clean if washed once after removing the Najasat. But if anything becomes Najis by urine it must be washed two times. It is better to wash two times even in the case of other najasats.

Clothes should be squeezed after every washing as described above. Still water which is just a kur or more than a kur, also, makes things clean in the same way.

These waters cannot become unclean by mere contact with Najasat. They will be unclean if either their taste, color or smell is changed by that contact.

One kur of water equals twenty-seven (27) cubic span in volume (3x3x3). It is better to make it 427/8 cubic span (31/2x31/2x31/2). (1 span =9 inch.)

Still water which is less than a kur becomes unclean by just coming into contact with a Najasat. To cleanse with clean still water, it is necessary to wash two times after removing the Najasat. It is even better to wash three times.

The water running from the pipes in the houses is treated as running water as long as it is flowing.

Pots must be cleansed three times with the water which is less than a kur, and once if it is washed in Kur or running water.

If a pig licks a pot, then it should be washed seven times whether the water is running or Kur or less than that.

The same is the rule if a rat dies in a pot.

If a dog licks the pot, it should be rubbed with wet, clean earth thoroughly; then, after washing away the mud, it should be washed twice with the water which is less than a Kur, or once in Kur or running water.

If a pot becomes Najis by liquor, it must be washed three times with running water as Kur. (It is better to wash it seven times.)

2. EARTH:
The earth cleanses the sole of the shoe or feet. But there are 3 conditions for it:

18

(a) Earth should be clean;

(b) Earth should be dry;

(c) If there is any Najasat on the sole of the feet, and it is removed by walking or rubbing on the earth, it becomes clean.

NOTE: This rule does not apply to the end of the stick or wheels of car or carts, etc.

3. SUN:

The sun cleans those things which cannot be moved like wall, tree, earth etc. If the Najasat is removed, and the place or tree, etc., is wet, and then it becomes dry by the direct rays of the sun, it becomes clean. If it dries by hot air, or by sun's heat without direct rays, it will still remain Najis.

4. ISTIHALA:

It means "change." If a Najis thing is changed into a clean thing (chemically), it will become clean. For example, if a dog after death is changed into earth, that earth will be clean.

THE GOLDEN HOLY MAUSOLEUM AND SACRED SHRINE OF IMAM ALI, (A.S.) Najaf Al Ashraf (Iraq).

5. INQILAB:

It is similar to Istihala. The difference is that in Istihala, the shape and form, all are changed, while in Inqilab, only the properties are changed, but the shape is not entirely changed. Its only example: If wine becomes vinegar it is Inqilab and it makes the vinegar clean.

NOTE: If grape juice is fermented, either by fire or by itself it is Haram (unlawful) to drink. But if that fermented liquid is boiled on fire and its two-thirds are evaporated, the remaining one third will become Halal.

6. INTIQAL:

It means to change place. If a mosquito sucks the blood of a man and there is a gap of time, so that the blood is called the blood of mosquito, it will become clean.

7. ISLAM:

Kafir becomes clean by accepting Islam.

LESSON 21
MUTAHHIRAT (II)

In previous lessons, seven Mutahhirat were explained. The remaining five are explained here:

8. TABA-IAT: means to follow. The following things become clean by it:

(a) When a Kafir becomes a Muslim, his minor children become clean automatically.

(b) If a well becomes Najis and the water is taken out of it until it becomes clean, then the wall of the well, the bucket and the rope will become clean automatically.

(c) While washing Najis things, our hands become unclean; but when that thing becomes clean, our hands become clean automatically.

(d) If wine becomes vinegar and thus becomes clean, the pot in which it was, will become clean automatically.

(e) Wood-plank or cement/stone slabs upon which the body of a dead Muslim is washed, as well as the piece of cloth used to cover his hidden parts, and also the hands of the person washing that body, become clean when the Ghusl-e-Mayyit is completed.

9. ZAWAL-E-AIN: If there is any Najasat on the body of an animal, it will become clean if that Najasat is removed or rubbed away from his body.

20

Likewise, the inner parts of human body, like mouth and nose, become clean if the Najasat is just removed from them. Eyelids, lips and dentures are not included in this rule.

10. ISTIBRA: The urine and stool of the animal which eats the refuse of man are Najis; and the only way of its Taharat is Istibra; i.e. preventing it from eating things that make it Najis for a certain prescribed period. This period is 40 days for camel; 30 days for cow; 10 days for sheep and goat; 5 or 7 days for duck; 3 days for hen.

If any of these animals is kept away from the refuse of man for the prescribed period, its urine and stool become Tahir, provided that, at the end of that period, they are no more called 'refuse-eating animals.'

11. GHAIBAT-E-MUSLIM: If there is a Muslim, who is a follower of the Shariat; and any of his clothes or things becomes Najis; then he goes out of your sight long enough to enable him to make it clean; then he comes back and you see him using that cloth in prayers, then you must believe that he has cleansed that cloth; otherwise, he would not have used it in prayers. It is called Ghaibat-e-Muslim, which means "Absence of Muslim."

12. FLOWING OF BLOOD: When a Halal animal is slaughtered according to the rules of Shariat, and its blood flows out of its body in such a quantity which is normal in that kind of animal, the blood which remains in its body becomes clean, but that blood which remains in those organs of body which are Haram (like spleen, bladder, etc.) must be avoided.

LESSON 22
RULES OF TOILET

While going to toilet, the following rules must be observed:

1. The place where one sits to urinate or to relieve bowels, must be such as to hide one's private parts from on-lookers.
2. It is Haram to urinate or relieve bowels in the following places:
(a) In the property of another person without permission of the owner;
(b) In a place which is Waqf for a certain group-for a person who is not from that group;
(c) On the grave of Muslims and in all places which are sacred in the religion, like Mosque, Imambara, etc.

21

3. It is Haram to face Qibla, or to keep the Qibla on the back when urinating or relieving bowels.

4. After urinating, the part of the body concerned must be washed twice (better, thrice) with water.

5. After relieving bowels, the part of the body concerned may be cleansed by water or alternatively with cloth, paper, or clay, provided the cloth, paper or clay itself is Tahir and dry, it is Wajib to use three separate pieces even if the body becomes clean before that. If after using the three pieces, the body is not clean, extra pieces should be used till the body becomes clean.

6. If the stool was mixed with some other Najasat (like blood), or the stool had spread outside the body (more than normal), or if some external Najasat had reached the part of the body concerned, then the only way of cleaning it is with water. Paper, etc., cannot make it Tahir.

7. It is better to use water after relieving bowels even when using paper, etc., is allowed.

8. It is Haram to use sacred things in cleaning the body after relieving bowels: for example, Khak-e-Shifa or a paper having the names of Allah or Masoomeen on it.

9. It is not allowed to use bone or dung in cleaning the body after relieving bowels.

LESSON 23
WUDU (WUZU) (ABLUTION)

Before saying any prayer, it is necessary to clean and wash some specified parts of the body to remove hadath i.e., uncleanliness or specified pollution. This act of cleaning which is technically called Wudu, must be performed in a prescribed manner. It consists of two parts,

    a. Sunnat, (optional)
    b. Wajib, (obligatory)

The Sunnat part of wudu consists of washing the hands up to the wrist twice, gargling thrice and rinsing the nostrils thrice.

The wajib part of wudu consists of:

1. Making the Niyyat (intention) in one's mind that the wudu is being performed for seeking closeness to Allah. If Niyyat is expressed in words, it should be read as follows:

22

"I perform wudu for the removal of hadath, and for offering my prayers, seeking closeness to Allah (Qurbatan ilal-lah)."

2. Washing the face once from the point where the hair of the head normally grows, down to the chin, and breadthwise as much of the face as comes between the outspread thumb and the middle finger of the hand. Washing once is wajib; washing twice is sunnat.

3. Washing the right arm, from the elbow down to the fingertips once, pouring the water always from top to bottom. If someone is wearing a ring, he should move it or remove it so that water can reach the entire surface of the skin.

4. Washing the left arm from the elbow to the fingertips once in the same manner as the right arm.
   Washing the arms once is Wajib; twice is sunnat.

5. Masah of the head. After washing the face and the hands, Masah of the head should be performed by drawing the wet fingers of the right hand from about the middle of the head up to the edge of the hair.

6. Masah of the feet should be performed by drawing the wet fingers of the right hand over the upper part of the right foot from the tip of the toes to the ankle, and then similarly, the left hand over the left foot.

All the above acts should be consecutive, and the order of sequence should be strictly followed.

When is Wudu (Ablutions) required?

Wudu is necessary for:

1. Salat (Prayer)
2. Tawaf-e-Wajib
3. Touching the writings of Quran and the names of Allah and the Fourteen Masoomeen.
4. Qada (Qaza) of Sajdah and Tashahhud.
5. To wash a copy of the Quran which has become Najis.
6. When it becomes Wajib because of Nazr, Ahad or Qasam.

NAWAQIZ-E-WUDU, i.e. those things after the occurrence of which Wudu becomes necessary if anyone wants to perform any Ibadat mentioned above. These are called Hadath as explained earlier. They are the following:

1. Urination
2. Defecation
3. Emission of flatus ex ano
4. Sleep
5. Losing consciousness, intoxication and all such things which affect the senses of a man.
6. Istihada (Istihaza) (in the case of women)
7. Janabat

LESSON 24
CONDITIONS OF WUDU (WUZU)

Following are the conditions for wudu (wuzu):

1. Tahir. The water of wudu must be Tahir (clean).
2. Mutlaq. The water of wudu must be pure (not mixed with anything).
3. Mubah. The water used for wudu, and the place where wudu is performed, must be mubah (lawful).
4. The pot containing water for wudu, should be mubah.
5. The container of water for wudu, should not be one made of gold or silver.
6. The face, hands, head and feet (which are called organs of wudu), must be Tahir (clean) at the time of wudu.
7. There must be sufficient time for wudu and prayer. It means that if the time of Salat is so short that if you begin wudu, the prayer will not be performed in time, then you should not do wudu. Instead you should perform Tayammum. But if the time needed for Tayammum is the same as that for wudu, then wudu should be performed.
8. Wudu should be performed with the intention of Qurbatan-Illallah, i.e., to obey the order of Allah, and to become nearer to Him. If it is performed to keep cool or with any other intention, the wudu will be Batil (void).
9. Tartib. Right sequence should be maintained in wudu. It means that you should begin by washing your face, then the right arm from the elbow down to the fingertips, then the left arm from the elbow down to the fingertips. Then you must do Masah of a part of your head, then the Masah of the feet. It is better to do the Masah of the right foot first, then

of the left foot but the Masah of both feet at the same time is also allowed.

10. Mawalat. It means that you must do all the above-mentioned acts in wudu without interruption - before the water on any part of wudu, becomes dry.

11. You must perform wudu yourself. If someone else washes your face or hands etc., or pours water on your face or hands, etc., your wudu will be Batil (void).

12. There should be no danger to your safety or to your health in using water for wudu.

13. There should not be anything on the organs of wudu which might prevent water from reaching them, such as a ring, or oil or nail polish etc.

LESSON 25
SALAT (PRAYERS)

The mandatory (Wajib) Salat (Prayers) are six in number. They are:

1. The Five Daily Prayers.
2. The prayer of Aayat, i.e. prayer when a solar or lunar eclipse takes place, or at the occurrence of earthquake or any other fear-inspiring natural calamity like cyclone etc.
3. The Funeral Prayer.
4. The prayer of Wajib Tawaf at the Kaaba.
5. The lapsed prayers of a father on his eldest son.
6. Those prayers which become mandatory when one has to fulfil Ijara, Nazr, 'Ahad and Vow.

Note: Friday Prayer is wajib-i-Takhyiri.

LESSON 26
TIMES OF PRAYERS

1. Subh (Fajr Prayer). Beginning from Subhe Sadiq, ending at sunrise.
2. Zuhr (Midday Prayer). Beginning from exact noon, ending when four Rakaats' time remains to sunset;
3. 'Asr (Afternoon Prayer). Beginning after completing of four Rakaats time from noon, ending at sunset;

4. Maghrib (Evening Prayer). Beginning after sunset when the reddish color at the horizons vanishes, ending when four Rakaats time remains to exact midnight.

5. 'Isha (Night Prayer). Beginning after completing of 3 Rakaats time from sunset, ending at midnight.

Note: If someone could not pray Maghrib and 'Isha because of some appreciable difficulty, he should pray both Salats before Subh (Fajr), without Niyyat of "Ada" or "Qada" (Qaza). Midnight is 12 hours after exact noon.

Some details about time:

1. Time of Fazilat: It is better to pray in the time of Fazilat when the prayers are rewarded with more thawab;

(a) Subh: From the Subh-e-Sadique up to the time when red color appears on the horizon;

(b) Zuhr: From the noon up to the time when the shadow of a given thing becomes equal to its lengh.

(c) Asr: After the time of Fazilat of Zuhr up to the time when the shadow of a given thing becomes double of its length;

(d) Maghrib: After sunset up to the time when the red color on the western horizon vanishes;

(e) 'Isha: After the time of Fazilat of Maghrib.

THE GOLDEN HOLY MAUSOLEUM OF IMAM HUSEIN (A.S.), the Grandson of the Prophet Muhammed (S.A.W.), Kerbela (Iraq).

26

2. Reserved and Joint times:
(a) Zuhr: Four Rakaats time after noon is the reserved time of Zuhr. If anyone prays Asr in that time, it will be Batil;
(b) Asr: Four Rakaats time before the sunset is the reserved time of Asr; if anyone prays Zuhr at that time, it will be Batil. The time between these two reserved times is the joint time of Zuhr and Asr;
(c) Maghrib: Three Rakaats time after sunset is reserved for Maghrib. If anyone prays Isha at that time, it will be Batil;
(d) 'Isha: Four Rakaats time before midnight is reserved for 'Isha; if anyone prays Maghrib in that time, it will be Batil. The time between the two reserved times is joint time of Maghrib and 'Isha.

LESSON 27
QIBLA

1. It is Wajib to face toward Qibla:
(a) While praying;
(b) and while slaugtering animals.
(c) It is also Wajib to face Qibla at the time of death and to keep the dead body facing Qibla at the times of:
(d) praying Namaz-e-Mayyit; (Prayer for Dead Person) and
(e) Burial.

NOTE: It is not Wajib to keep the dead body facing Qibla at the times of giving it Ghusl, Kafan or Hunut. But it is Mustahab (Ihtiyatan) to do so.

2. Qibla: Kaaba is Qibla for those who are in Masjidul-Haram and Masjidul-Haram is Qibla for the whole world. The whole space above Kaaba up to the sky, is Qibla.
3. If anybody does not know the exact direction of Qibla, he may ascertain it from the graves of Muslims, or Masajid, or may ask those who know the direction.
4. If a man does not know the direction and there is no way to ascertain Qibla, but has strong feeling that it must be in a certain direction, he should pray facing that direction.
5. If he has no idea at all, he is required to pray facing any one side though it is better to pray four times, facing four directions if there is enough time. If the time is not enough, then he may pray as many times as possible.

6. If he thinks that the Qibla must be in either of two directions, he must pray twice, facing both the directions.

7. If a man prays facing a certain direction, and after salat he comes to know that the difference was of 90 degrees or more, i.e. Qibla was on his right or left or back, he will have to repeat the prayer, if the time of that prayer has not lapsed. And it is better to recite its Qada (Qaza) if the time of the prayer has lapsed.

8. If in the above case, he comes to know that the difference was less than 90 degrees on either side, the prayer is not to be repeated.

9. It is unlawful to face Qibla, or to keep the Qibla on the back when sitting in toilet.

LESSON 28
CLOTH OF PRAYER

There are certain rules laid down concerning the clothes when saying prayers. They are:

1. The clothes must be Tahir (clean): The Salat on a Najis piece of cloth is Batil.

2. The cloth or clothes must be Mubah, not Ghasbi. Salat in a Ghasbi apparel is Batil. A piece of cloth bought with money from which Zakat or Khums (when Wajib) has not been paid, is Ghasbi, and Salat with such a cloth is Batil.

3. It should not be a part of an animal whose meat is Haram (unlawful). Therefore, hair of cats and such things are not allowed in Salat.

4. It should not be a part of any dead animal. Meat, hide and fat are supposed to be taken from dead body unless it is known that it has been taken from a Zabiha (lawfully killed animal). Therefore, leather belts or things like that are not allowed in Salat unless they are known to have been taken from a Zabiha, or have been purchased from a Muslim (provided it is known, or at least probable that the Muslim had purchased it after due scrutiny).

5. It is not allowed to pray in clothes which have sweat which came out during or after becoming unlawfully Junub.

6. It is not allowed to pray in clothes which have sweat of an animal which eats human excreta.

7. For men only. They should not wear anything made of gold - pure or mixed. But there is no harm in keeping gold in the pocket.

8. Men are not allowed to wear pure silk.

28

NOTE: Gold and pure silk are Haram (unlawful) for men at all times; not only when saying Salat. Men should not wear anything made of gold such as a wrist-watch, eyeglass frames, rings or chain - at any time. But women are allowed to wear gold and silk at all times.

OTHER RULES:

1. If a man did not know that his body or clothes were Najis, and came to know after the Salat, the Salat is correct.

2. If he knew that his body or clothes were Najis, and forgot and prayed in that cloth, he would have to pray again, if the time is still there, or pray Qada (Qaza) if there is no time.

3. If the cloth became Najis during Salat, and it was possible to change it or to clean it without disturbing the Salat, he should do it, and the Salat would be correct. If it is not possible to change or clean the cloth as mentioned above, and there is enough time, he should terminate the Salat, clean or change the cloth and pray afresh. If the time is not enough as mentioned above, and it is not possible to take away that cloth, he should proceed in the prayer in that cloth, and the Salat would be correct. The same rules apply if any part of his body becomes Najis during Salat. If he could take away the cloth, but had no other cloth, he should complete the Salat in that same cloth.

4. The following Najasats are forgiven in Salat:

(a) The blood which comes out of a wound or tumor, provided it is difficult to clean it or, at least change the bandage once a day. But if that blood reaches another part of the body which is far from that tumor or wound, it must be cleansed.

(b) The blood, (other than the blood of Haid (Haiz), Nafas, or Istihada (Istihaza), or of a dead body, or Kafir, or an animal whose meat is not Halal, on the cloth or body of the Namazi, which is less than 'Dirhame Baghalli' in area.

NOTE: Dirhame Baghalli is equivalent to the tip of the fore-finger.

(c) Those small wearing apparels which cannot be used to hide the Auratain (private organs of a human being) owing to their smallness, like small handkerchief, button, ring, etc., provided they are not made from Najasats. It is not allowed to keep these things in Salat even without wearing them.

(d) The clothes of the woman who rears an infant provided that:
The cloth has become Najis with the infant's urine; and she has no other cloth to change. In this case, she is allowed to clean the cloth once in a

day and then ignore the Najasat of his urine afterwards. This rule cannot be extended from the urine to other Najasats, or from the woman to man, nor from that woman who does not have another cloth to that one who has another cloth to change.

NOTE: The above-mentioned exceptions are for Najis cloths. It does not mean that other rules relating to a cloth made from dead body or from a part of an animal whose meat is not halal are also relaxed.

5. The rules about cloth concerning the Salat also apply in wajib Tawaf.

6. When there is no other cloth except Ghasbi, or golden, or silk, and he is obliged to wear it, owing to cold or because there are other persons, he may pray in it; but if he may take it off, he should pray, in a closed room, without cloth.

The same is the rule if there is no cloth other than Ghasbi or made from dead animal or from Haram animal.

If there is no cloth except a Najis one and it is not possible to cleanse it, he should pray wearing that same cloth and the Salat will be correct.

LESSON 29
PLACE OF A PRAYER

1. Salat is not allowed in a Ghasbi (somebody else's) place without his/her permission. The permission from the owner may be either explicit or implied.

If someone lives in a rented house and, for one reason or other, is prevented from paying the rent to the owner, then he should seek the owner's permission to live in that house without paying him any rent.

If the owner is not known, or his whereabouts are not known, then the property comes under the category 'Mal-e-Majhul-ul-Malik' (A thing the owner of which is not known). Such things become the property of Imam (A.S.), and in his Ghaibat, the Mujtahid has authority over such things.

Therefore, such cases should be referred to the Mujtahid for decision.

2. The place of Sajdah must be Tahir. Standing and sitting places, may be non-Tahir, provided there is no possibility of the Najasat extending to the body or the clothes of the person who is praying.

3. It is not allowed to pray in a place where the prayer cannot be completed properly, or where there is danger to the life, for example, on a busy road during rush hour.

4. The place of Salat should not be unstable, like springboard or foam, etc.

5. There should be enough space to stand properly and to perform Ruku and Sajdah properly.

6. If a man and a woman are praying in the same place, the woman must stand at least one span behind the man, or there should be a curtain or wall between them.

7. The place where the forehead is put in Sajdah should not be more than four fingers (about 2 1/2 inches) lower or higher than the place where toes and knees are put.

MASJID:

It is stressed that the Salat should be performed in a Masjid. Masajid in order of preference are:

(a) Masjidul-Haram (around Kaaba)--A prayer offered here is equivalent to 100,000 prayers offered anywhere else.

(b) Masjidun-Nabi (Madina)--A prayer offered here is equal to 10,000 prayers offered elsewhere.

(c) Masjidul-Kufa and Baitul-Muqaddas--A prayer offered in any of these Mosques is equivalent to a thousand prayers.

(d) Masjid Jame--A prayer offered here is equivalent to a hundred prayers.

(e) Masjid of the Market--A prayer offered here is equivalent to a dozen prayers.

For women, their home is better than the Masjid.

THE MAUSOLEUM OF IMAM MUSA AL KAZIM (A.S.) and IMAM TAQI (A.S.).

31

The Prophet (S.A.W.) has said: Three things will complain before Allah: (1) The Masjid which is neglected and nobody comes to pray there; (2) An Alim, among the people who do not know the religion and; (3) A Quran put in a place, from which nobody recites ever, and which remains covered with dust. Also, the Prophet (S.A.W.) has said: "There is no Salat for a neighbor of Masjid, but in Masjid."

Places where praying is Makrooh:

It is not proper to pray in a dirty place, or slaughter-house, or in a place where fire is burning, or when there is fire before him, or where there are photos of human beings or animals, or with open Quran before him, or any open book. It is also makrooh to pray in burial ground, or on a grave, or behind a grave, or between two graves, or where there is a human being facing him. It is makrooh to pray in Hammam, or on roads, or facing an open door or in a salty place, or in a room wherein someone is in Junub (Mujnib).

O' My Lord!
Make me and my children regular in prayer
O' Our Lord!
Accept my prayer
O' Our Lord!
Forgive me, my parents, and the Believers,
On the Day of Reckoning.
--Ibrahim: 40

LESSON 30
ADHAN (AZAN) AND IQAMAT

Saying Adhan (Azan) and Iqamat before starting daily prayers has great merit. They are given below.

ADHAN (AZAN)

ALLAHU AKBAR (Allah is the Greatest).
ALLAHU AKBAR
ALLAHU AKBAR
ALLAHU AKBAR

ASH-HADU ALLA-ILAAHA IL-LALLAH
     (I bear witness that there is no god but Allah.)
ASH-HADU ALLA-ILAAHA IL-LALLAH

ASH-HADU AN-NA MUHAMMEDER RASOOLULLAH
     (I bear witness that Muhammad is the Apostle of Allah.)
ASH-HADU AN-NA MUHAMMEDER RASOOLULLAH

*ASH-HADU AN-NA AMEERAL MOMINEENA ALIY YAN
HUJJATULLAH (I bear witness that the Commander of the Faithful,
     Ali is the Hujjat of Allah)
ASH-HADU AN-NA AMEERAL MOMINEENA ALI YAN
HUJJATULLAH

HAYYAY ALAS SALAAH (Hasten to prayer)
HAYYAY ALAS SALAAH

HAYYAY ALAL FALAH (Hasten to success)
HAYYAY ALAL FALAH

HAYYAY ALA KHAYRIL AMAL (Hasten to the best of deeds)
HAYYAY ALA KHAYRIL AMAL

ALLAHU AKBAR (Allah is the Greatest).
ALLAHU AKBAR

LAA ILAHA ILLALLAH (There is no god but Allah)
LAA ILAHA ILLALLAH

*These words should be said not as a part of Adhan (Azan) but for Barakat only.

IQAMAT

There is a slight difference between Adhan and Iqamat. While saying Iqamat, the words ALLAHU AKBAR at the beginning are to be repeated twice (and not four times). The words QAD QAMATISSALAH (Indeed the prayer has begun), are to be added after the words HAYYAY ALA KHAYRIL AMAL, and repeated twice; LAA ILAHA ILLALLAH at the end is to be said only once.

LESSON 31
WAJIBAT OF PRAYER

There are eleven things Wajib (obligatory) in the prayers, viz.,

1. Niyyat: the intention to pray, for being near to God.
2. Qiyam: to stand
3. Takbiratul-Ihram: saying Allaho-Akbar after Niyyat
4. Ruku
5. Two Sajdahs
6. Qira'at: To recite Sura Al-Hamd and another Sura in first two Rakaats and Tasbeehat-e-Arba'a (SUBHANALLAHE WAL HAMDU LILLAHE WA LA ILAHA ILLALAHO WALLAHO AKBAR) in the third and fourth Rakaats.
7. Dhikr: To recite Tasbeeh in Ruku and Sajdah (as will be explained later).
8. Tashahhud.
9. Salaam.
10. Tartib: To pray in the sequence prescribed by the Shariat.
11. Muwalaat: To pray without interruption or gap.

RUKN AND NON-RUKN:

Out of the above-mentioned Wajibs of Salat, 5 are Rukn and others non-Rukn.

Rukn means such actions which invalidate the Salaat if they are left out or added, even if unintentionally.

These are (1) Niyyat, (2) Takbiratul Ihram, (3) Qiyam at the time of Takbiratul Ihram and just before going to Ruku, (4) Ruku (5) both Sajdahs together. If any of these are left out, or added, whether intentionally or unintentionally, Salat will become Batil (wrong).

34

Non-Rukn means such Wajibs which invalidate the Salat if they are left out, or added, intentionally. But they do not invalidate the Salat if they are left or added unintentionally. These are the remaining Wajibs. (6th to 11th in the above).

LESSON 32
NIYYAT, TAKBIR AND QIYAM

1. NIYYAT: The person starting prayer must have, just before starting, a clear 'intention' that the specific prayer is 'Qurbatan Illallah,' i.e. for seeking nearness to Allah. Thus three things are Wajib in Niyyat:
   (a) The prayer must be specified;
   (b) It must be for the sake of God only, not for any other motive;
   (c) That intention must remain unaltered up to the end.
NOTE: It is not necessary to say these things in words. The intention and attention of the mind are enough.

2. TAKBIRATUL-IHRAM: The phrase 'Allaho Akbar' is called Takbiratul-Ihram, and it means "Imposition of limits." Thus, the 'Takbir' just after Niyyat is called 'Takbiratul-Ihram,' because it limits the man in his actions; now he cannot do any work except pray. There are 5 conditions in it:
   (a) It must be in the approved form, i.e. 'Allaho Akbar' without any addition or change and without joining it with other wordings.
   (b) It must be in correct Arabic.
   (c) It must be said while standing (details will come afterwards).
   (d) Body must be in 'Tamaninat' (not moving, but still).
   (e) Muwalaat: The letters and words should be recited one after another without gap.

3. QIYAM (STANDING): It is 'Rukn' while reciting 'Takbiratul-Ihram' and before going to 'Ruku'; and is Wajib (but not Rukn at the time of reciting Suras or Tasbihate-Arba'a. In Qiyam, it is Wajib that:
   (a) The person should stand erect, and face Qibla.
   (b) He should be motionless (Tamaninat).
   (c) Also he should not lean against anything unless he is unable to stand without support.

SUBSTITUTES OF QIYAM:
(a) If a man cannot stand without support, he should (or may) stand with support;
(b) If he cannot stand, even with support, he should sit without support;

35

(c) If he cannot sit without support, he may sit with support;
(d) If he cannot sit even with support, he must lie on his right side, facing Qibla;
(e) If it is not possible, he must lie on his left side facing Qibla;
(f) If even that is not possible, he should lie down on his back, his feet toward the Qibla.

In the last three alternatives, he should bow down for Ruku and Sajdah; the bowing for Sajdah should be more than that for the Ruku. If he cannot bow down, he should perform Ruku and Sajdah with his eyelids. If he can stand for a part of the prayer, he should stand up to that time, then should sit down. This rule applies to the alternatives also.

SUNNAT DIFFERENCES BETWEEN QIYAM OF MAN AND WOMAN:

Man stands with his feet apart from 4 to 8 inches; woman stands with her feet close to each other.

Man reaches his hands downwards resting on thighs; woman keeps her hands on her chest.

Man and woman both should keep their eyes (during Qiyam) on the place of Sajdah (Muhr).

LESSON 33
RUKU

4. **RUKU (Kneeling Down):** It is Wajib in each Rakaat once; except Salatul-Ayat which has 5 Rukus in each Rakaat.

There are five (5) Wajibs in Ruku:
(a) To bend so low that the palms rest on the knees;
(b) To recite 'Dhikr' of Ruku after bending up to the approved position.

Dhikr of Ruku: 'Sub-hanallah' (Glory be to Allah), 3 times, or 'Subhana Rabbiyal Azeeme Wabi Hamdehi' (Glory and Praise be to my Lord Cherisher, the Great) once.

(c) While reciting the Dhikr, one should remain motionless as far as possible.
(d) Standing again after Ruku, raising the head first;
(e) 'Tamaninat' in the Qiyam after Ruku.

These things are Sunnat in Ruku:

(a) Saying Takbir before kneeling down;

(b) Keeping the eyes fixed between the feet during Ruku;

(c) Reciting Dhikr 3, 5, or 7 times or even more.

(d) Reciting Salawat after Dhikr;

(e) Reciting 'Sami-Allaho leman hamedah' after standing erect after Ruku.

SUNNAT DIFFERENCES BETWEEN RUKU OF MAN AND WOMAN:

(a) A man must keep his palms on his knees; a woman on her thighs above the knees;

(b) A man should keep his fingers stretched on his knees; a woman should keep them joined together;

(c) A man should keep his arms and elbows away from the body, a woman should keep them joined to her body;

(d) A man should keep the knees stretched backwards, a woman should keep them not so tight;

(e) A man should keep his back in such a horizontal level that if a drop of water is dropped on the back it does not move down; a woman should keep her back in an arch fashion.

LESSON 34
SAJDAH (I)

5. *SAJDAH:* Each Rakaat has two Sajdahs, both taken as one Rukn.

Seven things are Wajib in Sajdah:

(a) One should prostrate so low that his forehead and feet are in one level.

(b) Seven parts of the body must be resting on the ground. These are the forehead, the two palms, the two knees and the toes of both feet.

(c) There are some special rules about the place of Sajdah:

(i) It must be either earth; or

(ii) Anything growing from earth, provided it is from those things which are not eaten or worn.

Therefore, Sajdah is not allowed on cloth or fruits or edible vegetables, or on such a thing which does not come under the term 'Earth' viz., diamond or gold, etc., or does not come under the term Vegetation viz., ash or coal.

Also, Sajdah is not correct on hide or skin, because it does not grow from the earth; nor is it allowed on carpets made of wool, cotton, jute or silk, because wool and silk do not grow from earth and cotton and jute are used in clothes.

Sajdah on paper is allowed.

Highest preference has been given to performing Sajdah on the earth from a specified area in Karbala. That earth is called 'Khake Shifa', ready-made tablets of which are available and are called 'muhr,' or 'turbat' or 'Sajdah-gah' in different languages.

The sajdagah must be clean. Dirty tablets are not allowed in prayers. Also, its size should not be less than your own thumb.

If there is nothing upon which Sajdah is allowed, or if there is so much cold or heat that he cannot put his forehead upon the earth, then, he may perform Sajdah upon the cloth. If there is no cloth then, as a last resort, it is allowed to perform Sajdah upon the back of his hand. Remember that mats in the mosques are made from a fibre which is neither eaten nor worn and it is quite in order to do Sajdah on them, especially if your forehead rests upon an uncolored portion. Likewise, you may do Sajdah on any stone (not precious stones); so you can do Sajdah on real (but not artificial) marble.

(d) To recite Dhikr of Sajdah, i.e. Sub-ha-nal-lah (three times) or Sub-hana Rabbiyal 'Aala wa Bihamdihi (Glory and Praise be to my Lord Cherisher, the High) once.

(e) To remain motionless during Dhikr of Sajdah.

(f) Not to raise any of the seven parts (mentioned in 5b) till the recitation of Dhikr is over.

(g) To raise the head first and sit down after first (and even second) Sajdah.

IMPORTANT REMINDER:

It is Haram in Islamic Shariat to perform Sajdah to anyone except Allah. Some ignorant people put their forehead in front of the graves of Imams (A.S.). If they have a clear intention to do Sajdah of Thanks (Sajdah-e-Shukr) for Allah, it is all right. Otherwise, it is Haram.

LESSON 35
SAJDAH (II)
MUSTAHABBAT OF SAJDAH

The following are Sunnat in Sajdah:
1. Keeping the nose also on earth.

2. During Sajdah, the hands must be in level with the ears and should point toward the Qibla. Fingers should be close to each other.
3. Eyes should see toward the nose.
4. Recitation of Dhikr more than once, as already explained in case of Ruku.
5. Recitation of Salawat after Dhikr.
6. After rising from first Sajdah, to say, first, Takbir, and then 'Astaghfirullaha Rabbi wa atubu ilaih.' (I seek pardon from Allah, my Lord and I turn toward Him). Then saying Takbir again before 2nd Sajdah.
7. To say Takbir after rising from second Sajdah while sitting.
8. Hands should rest, after rising from every Sajdah, on the thighs.
9. Recitation of 'Behaulillahe wa Qoowatehi Aqoomu wa Aq'ud' during the process of rising for the Rakaat.

Remember that it is the only place in the Salat when recitation of a Dhikr is prescribed during the motion of the body. All other Suras and Dhikrs must be recited when your body is motionless. (Meaning of this Dhikr: Due to the power given by Allah, and because of the strength given by Him, I stand and sit).

MAKROOHAT OF SAJDAH:

1. Sitting on heels (for men).
2. Keeping the arms on the ground during Sajdah.
3. Recitation of portions of the Qur'an in Sajdah.

Note: The above-mentioned five Wajibs (Niyyat, Takbirat-ul-lhram, Qiyam, Ruku and Sajdah) are Rukn. It means that if anyone of them is left out or added in Salat, by mistake or intentionally, the Salat is Batil.

SUNNAT DIFFERENCES BETWEEN SAJDAH OF A MAN AND THAT OF A WOMAN:

1. While stooping down for Sajdah, a man should lower his hands first but a woman should lower her legs first.
2. On arising from Sajdah, a man should sit on crossed feet, the back of right foot resting on the sole of the left, both feet turned out toward one side of the body. But a woman must sit on hams with the soles of the feet resting on the ground.
3. While rising for the next Rakaat, a man should keep first his hands on the ground, then raising the legs (before the hands) should stand. A

39

woman should keep her hands on her knees while sitting and should stand up straight from that position.
4. A man, while in Sajdah, should keep his arms apart from his body. A woman should keep her arms close to her body.

WAJIB SAJDAS OF QUR'AN

In four Suras of Qur'an (Alif Lam Meem Sajdah, Ha Meem Sajdah, Najm and Iqra) there is one ayat which is called ayat of Sajdah. Anybody who recites that Ayat or listens to it must do Sajdah at the end of that ayat. If while listening to it he was reciting it also, he should do two Sajdahs. The place where he does the Sajdah must be Mubah (not Ghasbi) and the place of forehead should not be more than 2₁/₂" lower or higher than the place of knees or toes. The rules about the things upon which Sajdah of Salat is allowed must be followed in this Sajdah also.

It is not Wajib to say any Dhikr in this Sajdah. Still it is Sunnat to recite the following Dhikr:

La-Ilaha-Illallaho Haqqan Haqqa; La-Ilaha-Ilallaho Imaanan wa Tasdiqua; La-Ilaha-Illallaho Ubudhiyyatan wa Riqqa; Sajadto laka ya Rabbe Taabbudan wa Riqqa; La Mustankifan wa la Mustakbiran; Bal ana Abdun Dhalilun Dhaifun Khaifun Mustajir.

It is not necessary to do Wudu (Wuzu) etc., or to face toward Qibla in this Sajdah.

LESSON 36
QIRA'AT

Now we come to those 6 Wajibs which are non-Rukn, i.e., if anyone of them is added or left out intentionally, the Salat would be Batil; but if it is added or left out by mistake or unintentionally, no harm will come to the Salat (except that some remedial actions are prescribed in certain cases).

6. QIRA'AT:
It is Wajib to recite Sura Al-Hamd and then any other Sura (with certain conditions) in the first two Rakaats of every Salat (except for Salat-e-Mayyit) and to recite either Tasbihate Arbaa (Subhanallahe

walhamdo lillahe wa la ilaha illallaho, wallaho Akbar) or Sura Al-Hamd in the third and fourth Rakaats.

Certain things are Wajib in the Qira'at:

(a) Correct pronounciation of the words and letters, so as the similar letters may be distinguished from each other in a correct way. This needs practice and training.

(b) Fat-ha, Kasra, Damma (Zamma), Tashdid, Madd and Jazm should be pronounced correctly.

(c) When stopping on a word, its last 'Irab' should be replaced by Jazm, compulsorily. Likewise, when two words are joined, the first word's Irab should not be omitted.

THE MAUSOLEUM OF IMAM ALI AR RAZA (A.S.) at Mashhad.

41

(d) Bismillahir-Rahmanir Rahim should be recited before every Sura except Sura al-Bara'at, because it is part of every Sura (except al-Bara'at).

(e) The four Suras in which Wajib Sajdahs occur, should not be recited in Wajib Salat.

(f) Reciting the Suras and Tasbihate Arbaa with Tamaninat (standing still and tranquil).

(g) A man should recite Al-Hamd and Sura loudly in the first two Rakaats of Subh, Maghrib and Isha; and in whisper in the first two Rakaats of Zuhr and Asr.

'Loudly' does not mean shouting. If someone prays so loudly that it may be said that he is 'shouting,' his prayer is invalid. The whisper should be audible to himself. The Qira'at in the 3rd and 4th Rakaats of every Salat should be in whisper.

A woman should recite her prayers in whisper, though she is allowed to pray loudly (where a man should pray loudly) when there is no danger that any Ghair-Mehram is nearby who may hear her voice. If someone intentionally prays loudly in place of "whispering," or vice-versa, his prayer is invalid.

(h) Reciting the Al-Hamd and Sura with Tartib (in the sequence which is prescribed).

(i) Muwalaat in the Qira'at.

(j) Sura Wad-duha (No.93) and Sura Alam Nashrah (No.94) are one Sura. Likewise, Sura Fil (No.105) and Sura Quraysh (No.106) are one Sura. If one of the Suras is recited, the other one should also be recited.

(k) A man who has started reciting any Sura after Al-Hamd, may change to other Sura so long as he has not reached the exact middle of that Sura. If he has, on the other hand, recited half of that Sura, he is not allowed to change it. But he cannot leave Sura Tauhid or Sura Kafirun even if he has just recited Bismillahir Rehmanir-Rahim with intention of reciting these Suras.

If he forgets any word or Ayat from the Sura which he is reciting, he may leave the Sura and start another one, even if he has already recited more than half or even if it is Sura Tauhid or Sura Kafirun.

(l) It is allowed to recite the Sura from looking into the Quran in Salat; but it is not good and one should not resort to it except in emergency when there is no time to learn by heart, nor is there any Salat-e-Jamaat to join.

LESSON 37
TRANSLATION OF 3 SURAS AND QUNOOT

(1) SURA-E-FATEHA (Chap. 1)

Bismillahir-Rahmanir-Rahim

In the Name of ALLAH, the Beneficent, the Merciful.

Al-Hamdu lillahi Rabbil Aalameen

(All) praise is to ALLAH the Lord Cherisher of the Worlds.

Ar-Rahmanir-Rahim

The Beneficent, the Merciful

Maliki Yaumiddin

The Master of the Day of Judgment.

Iyyaka Na'budu wa Iyyaka Nasta'een

Thee (alone) do we worship, of Thee only do we seek help.

Ehdinas-Sirratal-Mustaqeem

Guide us to the Straight Path.

Siraatal-lazeena An'amta Alaihim Ghairil Maghdubi Alaihim Waladdalleen

The path of those upon whom Thou hast bestowed (Thy) bounties; not of those on whom fell (Thy) wrath nor (of) those gone astray.

(2) SURA-E-QADR (Chap. 97)

Bismillahir-Rahmanir-Rahim:

In the name of ALLAH, the Beneficent, the Merciful.

Inna Anzalnaho fi Lailatil Qadr:

Verily, We sent it (the Holy Qur'an) down in the Night of Qadr.

Wa ma Adraaka ma Lailatul Qadr:

And what do thou know what the Night of Qadr is?

Lailatul Qadri Khairum min Alfi Shahr:

The Night of Qadr is better than a thousand months.

Tanazzalul Malaaikatu war-Rooho fiha be-izne Rabbihim min kulle amr, Salamun, hiya hatta Matla'il Fajr:

Descend in it the Angels and the Spirit with the permission of their Cherisher Lord with all Ordinances.
Peace...This until the rise of Morn .

43

(3) SURA-E-IKHLAS (Chap. 112)

Bismillahir-Rahmanir-Rahim: In the name of ALLAH, the most
Beneficent, the most Merciful.

Qul Howallaho Ahad: Say: He is God, the One and Only,

Allahus-Samad: God, the Eternal, Absolute

Lam Yalid: He begetteth not,

Wa Lam Yulad: Nor is he begotten;

Wa Lam Yakul Lahu Kufuwan
Ahad: And there is none like unto Him.

QUNOOT

It is Sunnat to recite Qunoot in the second Rakaat before Ruku. A short Qunoot (with translation) is given here:

Rabbanaghfir lana: O' Our Lord, Forgive us,

War-hamna: And have mercy on us,

Wa-Afena Waafu Anna: And give us tranquility; and
pass over our sins.

Fid-dunya wal-Aakhira: In this World and the Hereafter.

Innaka Alaa Kulle Shayyin   Verily, Thou hast Power over

Qadeer: everything.

LESSON 38
OTHER WAJIBAT

7. DHIKR:
Dhikr means the Tasbeeh of Ruku and Sajdah.

8. TASHAHHUD:
Tashahhud is Wajib after the second Sajdah of the second Rakaat and that of the last Rakaat. Six things are Wajib in it. They are:

(a) Reciting Shahadatain. It is recited as: "Ash-hado Alla Ilaha Illallaho Wahdahu la Sharika Lahu; Wa Ash-hado Anna Muhammadan Abdohu wa Rasuloh."

(b) Reciting Salawat after Shahadatain.

(c) Sequence in its sentences as explained above.
(d) Muwalat. (To pray without any interruption or gap).
(e) Reciting Tashahhud while remaining seated.
(f) Tamaninat. (One should be motionless).

MEANING OF SHAHADATAIN & SALAWAT

I bear witness that there is no god but Allah; the only One; there is no partner or equal to Him.
And I bear witness that Muhammad (S.A.W.) is His servant and His Apostle.
O Lord! Send Thy blessings on Muhammad (S.A.W.) and his progeny.

MUSTAHABBAT:
It is Mustahab in Tashahhud that the hands rest on the thighs. The fingers should remain close to each other pointing toward Qibla. Eyes should rest on the lap. The position of sitting for man and woman has already been described in the description of Sajdah.

9. SALAAM:
Salaam is Wajib after the Tashahhud of the last Rakaat. Four things are Wajib in it:
(a) Reciting either of these two sentences: "Assalamu Alaina wa'ala Ibadillahis Saleheen." (Peace be on us and all righteous servants of God). "Assalaamu alaikum wa Rahmatullahe wa Barakatuh." (Peace be on all of you and the Mercy of Allah and His Blessings).
(b) Remain sitting while reciting Salaam.
(c) Correct pronunciation.
(d) Tamaninat. (To be motionless).

MUSTAHABBAT:
(a) Reciting both Salaams.
(b) Addition of "Assalaamu Alaika Ayyuhan Nabiyu wa Rahmatullahi wa barakatuh." (Peace be on thee, 0 Prophet and the Mercy of Allah and His Blessings).   (c) Saying Takbir three times after Salaam.

45

10. TARTIB: (Sequence)

It is Wajib to perform all the acts of prayer (Salat) in the prescribed sequence. Any change in that sequence will invalidate the Salat if done intentionally (and in case of a Rukn's sequence, even unintentionally).

11. MUWALAAT: (To pray without any interruption or gap)

One act of prayer must be followed by the next act immediately. The intervening time between two acts should not be so long as to give the impression that the person concerned is not praying any more.

THE MAUSOLEUMS AT SAMARRA. Beneath the Golden Dome are the graves of Imam Ali Alnaqi (A.S.), Imam Hassan Al Askari (A.S.).

LESSON 39
THE ACTIONS WHICH INVALIDATE PRAYER:

There are certain things or actions which invalidate a prayer:

1. Hadath whether big or small, and whether intentionally or by mistake.
2. Turning away from Qibla.
3. Anything which disturbs the prayer (i.e. anything which gives the impression that the person is not praying), like remaining silent for a considerable time, clapping the hands or jumping or indulging in actions other than the prayer.
4. Speaking intentionally even a single letter (other than prayer or Qur'an or Dhikr of Allah). But replying to Salaam-e-Shar-ee ('Salaamun Alaikum') is allowed in the very same words.
5. Laughing intentionally. Smiling does no harm to the prayer.
6. Weeping intentionally for worldly affairs. But weeping in love or fear of Allah does no harm to the prayer.
7. Eating or drinking, however little it may be, whether intentionally or by mistake.
8. Folding the hands intentionally as some non-Shia sects do in the prayer.
9. Saying 'Amin' intentionally after Sura Al-Hamd.
10. If any of the conditions of prayer is violated. For instance, he realizes during prayer that his cloth is Ghasbi (possessed unlawfully).
11. Doubt in first two Rakaats of a four Rakaat prayer, or anywhere in a two Rakaat or three Rakaat prayer.
12. Adding or leaving out any Rukn of prayer.

LESSON 40
SHAKKIYAAT (DOUBTS OCCURRING IN PRAYERS)

Even though we pray with concentration and due attention, there are times when some doubts arise as to whether we performed a particular part or we missed it. In such cases, one should ponder for a moment to clear one's mind. If the doubt is removed, well and good. If not, one should act in accordance with guidelines as under.

There are 23 cases of Shakkiyaat (Doubts) that may arise during Salat. The Laws of Shari'at are distinct for each one of these.

47

DOUBTS (SHAKKIYAAT) TO BE IGNORED

There are six instances in which doubt is to be ignored. Prayer is not made invalid by any of these. They are:

1. Doubt after the time has passed, e.g., doubt in Ruku if one has read Al-hamd or not.
2. Doubt after completing the prayer.
3. Doubt after the time of prayer has passed.
4. Doubt of the people who doubt too much.
5. The doubt of the Imam in the number of Rakaats when the Mamum (the follower) knows the right number; or the doubt of the Mamum while the Imam knows the right number.
6. Doubt during the non-obligatory (Sunnat) or precautionary (Ehtiyat) prayer.

LESSON 41
DOUBTS THAT REQUIRE REMEDIAL PROCEDURE

There are nine cases that require remedial procedures to be carried out to validate the prayers.

1. When one doesn't know, after the second Sajdah, if one has read two Rakaats or three, then he should assume that he has read three Rakaats; he should read one more Rakaat, and complete the Salat. Thereafter, he should offer one Rakaat precautionary (standing) prayer.

2. When one doesn't know, after the second Sajdah, if one has read two Rakaats or four, he should assume that he has read four Rakaats, and should complete the Salat. Thereafter, he should read two Rakaat prayer, precautionary (standing).

3. When one doesn't know, after the second Sajdah, if one has read two Rakaats or three or four, then he should assume that he has read four Rakaats. He should complete the prayers, and then he should read two Rakaats prayer standing, and two Rakaats sitting, precautionary.

4. When one doesn't know, after the second Sajdah, if one has read four Rakaats or five, he should assume that he has read four Rakaats. He should complete the prayer, and then he should perform two Sajdah-e-Sahv.

In the case of these four doubts, if any one of them occurs after the first Sajdah or before the Dhikr of the second Sajdah, then the prayer is invalid.

5. When during the prayer, one has doubt if he has read three or four Rakaats, then he should assume that he read four Rakaats; he should complete the prayer, and then read Salat of Ehtiyat, one Rakaat standing or two Rakaats sitting.

6. When during Qiyam, one has doubt about the number of Rakaats, four or five, then he should sit down, read Tashahhud, and Salam, and complete the prayer. Then he should read Salat of Ehtiyat, one Rakaat standing or two Rakaats sitting.

MAUSOLEUM OF HAZRAT ABBAS (A.S.) at Kerbela (Iraq).

49

7. When during Qiyam, one has doubt about the number of rakaats, three or five, he should sit down, read Tashahhud, read Salam, and complete the prayer. Then he should read Salat of Ehtiyat, two Rakaats standing.

8. When during Qiyam one has doubt about the number of Rakaats, 3, 4 or 5, he should sit down, read Tashahhud and Salam, and complete the prayer. Then he should read Salat-e-Ehtiyat, two rakaats standing; and then two Rakaats sitting.

9. When during Qiyam one has doubt in the number of Rakaats, 5 or 6, he should sit down, read Tashahhud and Salam; perform two Sajdah-e-Sahv. Then as Ehtiyat Wajib, in these last four cases, he should perform two more Sajdah-e-Sahv.

LESSON 42
DOUBTS THAT INVALIDATE PRAYER

Those doubts which invalidate a prayer, are as follows:

1. In obligatory prayers of 2 Rakaats (Salat of Fajr and Salat of Musafir), if one has doubt in the number of Rakaats, the Salat is void. But such does not invalidate a non-obligatory or precautionary prayer.

2. Doubt in the number of Rakaats in a prayer of three Rakaats.

3. When one has a doubt in a 4-Rakaat prayer, if he has read one or more than one Rakaat.

4. When one has a doubt in a 4-Rakaat prayer, before completing the Dhikr of the second Sajdah, if he has read two Rakaats or more.

5. Doubt between 2 and 5 Rakaats, or between 2 and more than five Rakaats.

6. Doubt between 3 and 6 Rakaats or more than six Rakaats.

7. Doubt in the number of Rakaats; i.e., one does not know how many Rakaats he has read.

8. Before or after completing the second Sajdah, if there is doubt between 4 and 6 or more than 4 and 6 Rakaats.

LESSON 43
PRAYER OF EHTIYAT AND SAJDAH-E-SAHV

SALAT OF EHTIYAT:

You have been taught that in the case of some doubts about the number of the Rakaats of Salat, you have to pray one and/or two Rakaats Salat-e-Ehtiyat. Here is how that Salat is prayed.

Soon after finishing the Salat (in which the doubt had occurred and which requires Salat-e-Ehtiyat for its completion and validation) without looking away from Qibla or doing anything which makes a Salat Batil, you are to stand up and make the Niyyat. (If the Salat-e-Ehtiyat is to be performed sitting, then remain seated after the first Salat and make Niyyat).

Niyyat is to be made in the following way: "I pray Salat-e-Ehtiyat one (or two) Rakaat(s) Wajib Qurbatan Ilallah." Then Takbirat-ul-Ihram; recite only Sura Al-Hamd in whisper. Go to Ruku, and then into Sajdah; read Tashahhud and Salaam. Your Salat-e-Ehtiyat is finished.

Note: In Salat of Ehtiyat, there is no second Sura and no Qunoot. One should read this Salat quietly. One should not make the Niyyat also loudly or audibly. It is Ehtiyat Wajib that one should read Bismillah also quietly.

If you have to recite two Rakaats of Salat-e-Ehtiyat, then you should stand up for the second Rakaat just after the second Sajdah for the first Rakaat in the usual way. Recite the second Rakaat also with just Sura Al-Hamd, without Qunoot, and then finish the Salat in the usual way.

SAJDAH-E-SAHV:

Sajdah-e-Sahv is Wajib when:-
1. One talks unintentionally during the Salat.
2. One reads Salam at the wrong place, e.g., reading Salam after the first Rakaat.
3. One omits Tashahhud from Salat out of forgetfulness.
4. To doubt, in a 4-Rakaat Salat, after the Dhikr of second Sajdah if one has read 4 or 5 Rakaats.
5. To forget one Sajdah, or to sit down when one should be standing, e.g., when reading Al-Hamd or Sura; or to stand up when one should be seated, e.g., when reading Tashahhud. In all these 3 cases, for reasons of Ehtiyat (precaution), one should perform two Sajdahs of Sahv. In fact, one should perform two Sajdah-e-Sahv for every case when one has done something more or something less than what is actually prescribed.

51

HOW TO PERFORM SAJDAH-E-SAHV:

Soon after completing the Salat, Niyyat should be made as follows: "I perform Sajdah-e-Sahv in lieu of Tashahhud (or Salam or Sajdah or Qiyam etc., as the case may be) Wajib Qurbatan Ilallah." Then Sajdah should be done. In Sajdah you have to say once "Bismillahe wa billahe Assalaamu Alaika Ayuhhan-Nabiyyu wa Rahmatullahe wa barakatuhu." Then raise your head; sit properly; go into Sajdah a second time; recite the above-mentioned Dhikr once; sit down properly; read Tashahhud, and say "Assalamo Alaykum wa Rahmatullah wa Barakatuhu".

If you have forgotten Tashahhud or one Sajdah in the Salat, it is Wajib to do its Qada (Qaza) at once after Salat; then the Sajdah-e-Sahv is to be done just after the Qada (Qaza) Tashahhud or Sajdah.

If after the prayer, but before the Qada (Qaza) of Sajdah or Tashahhud, any of such actions is done which invalidate the prayer (like turning away from Qibla), it is necessary to do the Qada (Qaza) and Sajdah-e-Sahv (as required), and then to repeat the prayer.

LESSON 44
GHUSL (BATH)

1. Seven kinds of Ghusl are Wajib:
(1) Janabat, (2) Haid, (3) Nifas, (4) Istihada, (5) Mayyit, (6) Mass-e-Mayyit, (7) the Ghusl of Nazar, Qasam or Ahd.
2. How to perform Ghusl:
There are two ways of performing Ghusl: (1) Tartibi (Systematic) and (2) Irtimasi (Immersion).

GHUSL-E-TARTIBI: (SYSTEMATIC)

In this way of Ghusl, the body is washed in three stages. First, the head down to the collar bone is washed, including the face and neck. Second, the right side of the body is washed from the shoulders down to the feet. Third, the left side of the body is washed likewise. This Ghusl is preferable, even if you are bathing in a pool or river or sea. In bathroom, no method can be used other than the Tartibi Ghusl.

GHUSL-E-IRTIMASI: (IMMERSION)

1. If one has the intent of performing Ghusl Irtimasi, and he enters the water by degrees, and his whole body goes under water, his ghusl is correct. But it is better that he dives into the water.

2. In this ghusl, once the whole body is under water, and if one moves the body after making niyyat for ghusl, his ghusl is correct. In ghusl-e-Irtimasi, the whole body should be clean (pak) before one enters the water. But in Ghusl Tartibi, it is not essential that the body should be clean. If the body is najis, and one removes the impurity before washing each part, it is correct.

3. All those conditions which are essential to make a wudu correct, e.g., the water should be clean, and should be mubah etc., are also essential to make a ghusl correct. However, it is not essential that in ghusl, the body should be washed from top downwards. In ghusl tartibi, it is not essential that after washing one part, the other part should be washed immediately. If someone washes the head and neck, then pauses, then washes the right side, and then after an interval, washes the left side, it is acceptable. If someone has to urinate or defecate very frequently, and he has very limited time, he should wash first one part and then immediately the other, and after ghusl, he should say his prayer. Same rule is applicable to a woman who has Istihada. (to be explained later).

4. If a man is under obligation to perform several ghusls, he can make niyyat for all of them, and take only one ghusl. He can also take ghusl separately for each of them.

5. If a man has done ghusl-e-janabat, he does not have to perform wudu for prayer. But if he has done some other ghusl, then he cannot say prayer just with that ghusl. He will have to take wudu also.

LESSON 45
GHUSL OF JANABAT

1. WHEN REQUIRED?
There are two things which cause "Janabat" and it is Wajib to perform Ghusl of Janabat after them:
(a) Discharge of semen in sleep or while awake.
(b) Sexual intercourse. (Both parties become mujnib).

2. WHY REQUIRED

Ghusl is Wajib for all the things for which Wudu (Wuzu) is required. Also, it is Wajib to validate a Som (fast), as will be explained later.

3. THINGS WHICH ARE HARAM (FORBIDDEN) BEFORE GHUSL-E-JANABAT:

The following things are Haram, if a person has to perform Ghusl-e-Janabat:

(a) Reciting even a single Ayat from those Suras in which Sajdah is Wajib;

(b) Touching the writings of the Qur'an or the names of Allah, Prophets (A.S.), or Imams (A.S.) (in any script);

(c) Entering any mosque. (If necessary, he/she may pass through the mosque without stopping for a single second).

But so far as the mosque of the Prophet (S.A.W.), at Medina and Masjid-ul-Haram, at Makkah, are concerned, even passing through them is not allowed;

(d) putting anything into a mosque even from outside; and entering into a mosque to take out anything.

NOTE 1: *The Shrines of Imams (A.S.) are like the mosques in every detail.*

4. THINGS WHICH ARE MAKROOH IN THE JANABAT:

For a person who is to perform Ghusl-e-Janabat, it is makrooh to

(1) read Qur'an more than seven Ayats. (This applies to the Suras in which no Sajdah is Wajib);

(2) touch the Qur'an (but not touch the writing); it is Haram to touch the writing when one is junub.

(3) carry Qur'an from one place to another, even without touching it.

LESSON 46
GHUSL OF HAID (HAIZ) AND NIFAS
(A) HAID (HAIZ)

"Haid" means "menstruation", generally known as 'monthly course' or 'periods'. Every adult and healthy woman has her periods regularly. Shariat has laid down some rules for this period, a summary of which is given here:

1. Any blood seen before completion of 9 years or after 50 years of age is not "Haid." It is called "Istihada," rules of which will be explained later on.

2. Duration of "Haid" is not less than 3 and not more than 10 days. Blood which comes for less than 3 days, or which comes after 10 days, is called "Istihada."

3. There are detailed rules concerning women which are based on whether in condition of Haid (Haiz) she has regular date and/or number of days or not; and whether she is having her period for the first time, or whether she has forgotten her date and number of days.

As it is not possible to give all details here, the ladies are advised to consult a local Alim.*

* Note: On this subject, ladies may refer to a book called "The Ritual Ablutions for Women," by Maulana Sayyed Muhammad Rizvi.

THE MAUSOLEUMS AT SAMARRA. Beneath the Blue Dome is the Sardab (Cellar) where the Imam Mehdi (A.S.) is said to have disappeared.

(B) NIFAS

The bleeding after childbirth is called Nifas. The blood coming out before the delivery is not Nifas; it is Istihada.

The bleeding after 10 days from delivery is not Nifas; it is Istihada. But there is no minimum time for Nifas. Even if it stops 5 minutes or less after delivery, it is Nifas.

(C) THINGS WHICH ARE HARAM IN HAID (HAIZ) AND NIFAS

1. All the things which are Haram in the condition of Janabat are Haram in the condition of Haid and Nifas, before performing the Ghusl. Likewise, all the things Makrooh in Janabat are Makrooh in Haid (Haiz) and Nifas also.
2. In addition, it is forbidden to divorce a woman in the period of Haid (Haiz) or Nifas.
3. Sexual intercourse is forbidden when a woman is in menstruation or Nifas.
4. The woman during Haid (Haiz) or Nifas is exempted from prayers, and every such 'Ibadat' which requires Ghusl, Wudu (Wuzu), or Tayammum, but she may recite Dua, etc. (without touching the writings of the Qur'an or the names of Allah, Prophets (A.S.), or Imams, (A.S.) which is Haram for her as mentioned earlier). She is not required to pray Qada (Qaza) of the prayers left during the period of Haid (Haiz) and Nifas.
5. A woman in Haid (Haiz) or Nifas cannot fast; but she must fast its Qada (Qaza) after that period.

LESSON 47
ISTIHADA (ISTIHAZA)

The vaginal bleeding which doesn't fall under the category of Haid (Haiz) and/or Nifas is termed Istihada. Depending upon the extent of bleeding it is further divided into:

1. Istihada Qalila (Minor Istihada): If the blood doesn't penetrate the Sanitary napkin (or cotton pad used for protection, it is minor Istihada.

In this case, the Ghusl (ceremonial bath) is not needed. But she is supposed to perform Wudu (Wuzu) for each prayer. She is not allowed to pray two prayers with one Wudu (Wuzu).

2. Istihada Mutawassita (Medium Istihada): if the blood penetrates the cotton pad but does not exceed it, it is medium Istihada. For a woman with medium Istihada, one Ghusl (ceremonial bath) is obligatory for each day she bleeds. She should perform Wudu (Wuzu) for each prayer. To illustrate, if she starts bleeding before Zuhr, she should perform Ghusl before Zuhr, then perform a Wudu (Wuzu) for Zuhr prayer, and a Wudu (Wuzu) for each prayer thereafter till the next day, when she should perform a Ghusl before Zuhr.

3. Istihada Kathira (Major Istihada): When the bleeding is profuse, soaking the pad and exceeding it, it is Major Istihada. A woman with Major Istihada should perform Wudu (Wuzu) for each prayer. She should also take the ceremonial bath thrice a day, one before the morning prayer (Fajr), another before mid-day prayer (Zuhr) and yet another before the evening prayer (Maghrib).

SOME IMPORTANT CONSIDERATIONS:
1. It is necessary to change cotton pad before each Wudu (Wuzu).
2. If a woman is unable to perform Wudu (Wuzu) or take the ceremonial bath due to any permissible reason as discussed in the next lesson, she should perform Tayammum in place of Wudu (Wuzu) and/or Ghusl.
3. When a woman follows the above-mentioned rules, she should not consider herself as Najis, she will be Tahir.

LESSON 48
TAYAMMUM

I. *When to do Tayammum:*

1. When there is no possibility of finding water sufficient for Ghusl or Wudu (Wuzu);
2. When owing to old-age or the danger of thieves or beasts or unavailability of any means to get water from its place it is difficult to do Ghusl or Wudu (Wuzu);
3. When there is any danger to life or health from the use of water;
NOTE: If by using hot water, that danger can be averted, then it is necessary to use hot water; Tayammum is not allowed.
4. When there is water, but one is afraid that by using that water he will put himself, his companions or valuable animals in the danger of remaining thirsty or becoming ill;

5. When there is water but the body or the cloth of the person concerned is Najis (unclean), and he finds that if he uses the water in Wudu (Wuzu) or Ghusl, his body or the cloth will remain Najis. In this case, he will cleanse his body or the cloth by water and then will perform Tayammum;

6. When there is no water except Ghasbi or Mudaf (Muzaf) or there is no pot of water except a pot which is made of silver or gold or which is Ghasbi;

7. When the time of prayer is so short that if he starts Wudu (Wuzu) or Ghusl, his prayer will be Qada (Qaza) and he expects that by doing Tayammum the prayer will be completed in time.

In these seven conditions, a person should perform Tayammum.

II. *Things upon which Tayammum is permissible:*

Tayammum should be performed (in order of preference) on:
(a) Earth; (b) Sand; (c) Chunks of sand or earth - other than baked in fire; (d) Stones - other than minerals; (e) If the first mentioned four things are not available, then and only then, it is permissable to do Tayammum on the dust which accumulates upon the mats, floors, desks, etc.;

NOTE: Some people keep earth in a small bag and do Tayammum when necessary,upon the dust which gathers on the outside. It is not correct. They have EARTH with them. Therefore, they are not allowed to do Tayammum on dust which has been allowed only as an emergency measure. They should open the bag and do Tayammum on earth.

III. *The conditions about the above-mentioned things:*

1. All the above-mentioned things must be dry as far as possible. Even the mud should be dried, if possible, to convert it into a chunk of earth;

2. They must be Tahir (clean); and

3. Mubah and not Ghasbi (with permission of the owner);

4. The place where these things are kept, must be Mubah; (must have permission of the owner);

5. The place where you are standing while doing Tayammum, must be Mubah (with permission of the owner).

IV. *How to do Tayammum:*

The following four things are mandatory in Tayammum:
1. Niyyat. One must make Niyyat as follows: I am performing Tayammum instead of Wudu (Wuzu) or Ghusl (as the case may be), so that my prayer

(Salat) or fast (Som) may be correct, Wajib or Sunnat (as the case may be) Qurbatan Ilallah.

2. Strike the palms of both hands together upon the thing on which Tayammum is correct, such as earth or sand etc. Remember that just putting the hands upon earth etc., is not sufficient. You must hit or strike it by your palms.

3. Pull both palms together from the beginning of the forehead down to the point of the nose. Both sides of the forehead should be included in it. Eyes and cheeks are not to be included.

4. Then pull the left palm upon the back of the right hand from the projecting small bone on the joint of palm and arm to the fingertips. Do the likewise on the back of the left hand.

Whether Tayammum is performed instead of Wudu (Wuzu) or Ghusl, there is no difference in it.

LESSON 49
PRAYER OF AYAAT (SIGNS)

1. Its causes:

The prayer of "Signs" (Ayaat) is Wajib when any of the following signs occurs:

(a) Solar Eclipse.

(b) Lunar Eclipse.

(c) Earthquake.

(d) Any natural occurrence which normally creates fear in the common people, like black, red or yellow storm, cyclone and things like that.

2. Its time:

In Solar and Lunar Eclipse, the time of the "prayer of Signs" is from beginning of the eclipse till it is completely cleared.

In other cases like earthquake, it must be prayed soon after the cause subsides. But it is always performed with niyyat of Ada, even if prayed many days after its occurrence.

3. Its method:

Prayer of Signs is 2 Rakaats; every Rakaat has 5 Ruku (Total 10 Ruku).

After Niyyat and Takbiratul-Ihram, you should recite Sura Al-Hamd, then any other Sura; then go into Ruku. Your one Ruku is complete. After rising from Ruku, recite again Sura Al-Hamd and one Sura and go to Ruku. Your second Ruku is complete. Likewise, you should do 5

59

Ruku. After rising from 5th Ruku, say 'Sami-Allaho Leman Hamedah' and go into Sajdah. Complete 2 Sajdahs as usual and rise for the 2nd Rakaat.

Likewise, do 5 Ruku in the 2nd Rakaat, and perform 2 Sajdahs, recite Tashahhud and Salam as usual. Your prayer is complete.

NOTE: It is Sunnat to recite Qunoot before every second Ruku. For this purpose, count all ten Ruku together. Thus, you will recite Qunut before 2nd, and 4th (in first Rakaat), and before 6th, 8th and 10th Ruku (in 2nd Rakaat).

4. Short Method:

Also, you are allowed to pray this prayer by a short method:

After Takbiratul Ihram, you recite Sura Al-Hamd, and only a verse of a sura; then go to the first Ruku, after rising recite another subsequent verse of that sura and go to second Ruku, rise again and recite the third subsequent verse of that sura and go to the 3rd Ruku. Likewise, do before 4th and 5th Ruku, finishing the sura before 5th Ruku, e.g., Sura Ikhlas (Chapter 112).

THE DOME OF ROCK, (Jerusalem) (Beit-ul-Muqqaddas).

60

For example: Sura Qul-Hu-Wallah has 5 ayats. You may recite 'Bismillahir-Rahmanir-Rahim' before first Ruku; 'Qul-Hu-Wallahu Ahad' before 2nd Ruku; 'Alla-hus-Samad' before 3rd Ruku; 'Lam Yalid wa lam yulad' before 4th Ruku; and 'Lam Yakul-Lahu Kufuwan Ahad' before 5th Ruku.

Thus you would have read only one Al-Hamd and only one complete Sura in one Rakaat. You may recite one Rakaat in one way and the other Rakaat in the other way.

LESSON 50
FRIDAY PRAYER

In the presence of Imam (A.S.) or his specially appointed authority, Friday prayer is Wajib-e-Ayni in place of Zuhr. Zuhr is not recited on such occasions.

In ghaibat of Imam (A.S.) when there is no one specially appointed by Imam (A.S.) to lead in this prayer, Friday prayer and Zuhr become Wajib-e-Takhyiri.

Wajib-e-Takhyiri means that a man has an option to choose between two 'Wajibs,' but he cannot leave both. For example, in the 3rd and 4th Rakaat of daily prayers, a man has to recite either 'Tasbihat-e-Arbaa' or Sura Al-Hamd. He has to choose anyone of these two alternatives, but cannot leave both. Thus these two things are "Wajib-e-Takhyiri" in these two Rakaats.

Likewise, on Fridays, Zuhr and Friday prayer are Wajib-e-Takhyiri. It means that a man has the option to choose between these two prayers. But he cannot omit both.

There are certain conditions for Friday prayer:
1. Friday prayer must be prayed in Jamaat.
2. There must be at least 5 (better 7) persons including Imam.
3. Only one Friday prayer may be prayed in a radius of 3 miles 720 yards. If two prayers are held within this distance, the latter will be null and void.
4. There must be two sermons delivered by the Imam before the prayer and attentively listened to by at least 4 (or 6) persons.
5. As explained earlier, it is not Wajib to hold Friday prayers specially. Instead, Zuhr may be prayed. But if Friday prayer is held by an Aadil Imam, then it is Wajib (Ihtiyat Wujubi) to participate in that prayer; and there will be no need to pray Zuhr afterwards.
6. Friday prayer is two Rakaats: In the first Rakaat it is sunnat for the Imam to recite Sura Juma and in the 2nd Rakaat Sura Munafiqoon, after Sura-Al-Hamd.

7. Two Qunoots are Sunnat in this prayer: In the lst Rakaat before Ruku; in the 2nd Rakaat after rising from Ruku. There is a special Qunoot for Friday.

"Allahumma Inna Abidam min Ibadikas Saleheena Qamu bikitabika wa Sunnati Nabiyyeka Fajzehim Anna khairal-jaza." (0 Allah, verily, some servants from among Thy pious servants stood firm with Thy Book and the traditions of Thy Prophet; Thou reward them with the best Reward from us.).

LESSON 51
EID PRAYERS

The Muslims observe two big festivals each year. One is Eid-ul-Fitr and the other is Eid-ul-Adha. These two are the days of great festivity.

'Eid-ul-Fitr' is observed at the end of the holy month of Ramadan. Fasting creates the feelings of faith, spirituality, patience, contentment, and sacrifice. The festivity of the Muslims is not akin to dancing, singing songs or playing games. We submit ourselves to Allah offering Eid prayer for those religious, spiritual and moral benefits which accrue to us during the holy month of Ramadan.

'Eid-ul-Adha' is observed on the lOth of Dhil-Hijja, the day when Prophet Ibrahim (A.S.) intended to sacrifice his son Ismail in obedience to Allah's command. The Holy Qur'an has narrated the whole episode, which is the greatest example of self-sacrifice. The festival of Adha is in remembrance of this sacrifice. It reminds us that all our possessions, everything we have, including our lives and of those near and dear to us, should be sacrificed in the way of Allah, if necessary. Again, we offer the special prayer - Eid prayer.

Eid prayer is Sunnat, not Wajib, in these days when our Imam (A.S.) is hidden from us. The Niyyat of Eid prayer should be done as follows:

I pray two Rakaat of 'Eid-ul-Fitr' (or 'Eid-ul-Adha') Sunnat Qurbatan Ilallah."

In the first Rakaat, after Sura Hamd, Sura A'ala (87th Sura) is recited, then hands are raised for Qunoot.

DU'A-E-QUNOOT

"Allahumma ahlal Kibriyae wal azamah wa ahlal juude wal jabaroot, wa ahlal afwe warrahmah, wa ahlattaqwa wal maghfirah; asaloka behaqqe haazal yaumil lazi ja'altahu lil Muslimeena 'eedan, wa le Muhammadin Sallallaho alaihe wa Aalehi zukhran wa karamatan wa sharafan wa mazeeda; an tusalleya 'ala Mohammadin wa Aale Mohammadin, wa an Tudkhelani fi kulle khairin adkhalta fihe Mohammadan wa Aala Mohammadin, wa an Tukhrijani - min kulle soo-in Akhrajta minho Mohammadan wa Aala Mohammadin, Salawaatoka 'alaihe wa 'alaihim ajma'een. Allahumma, inni as'aloka khaira ma sa-a-laka behi ibadokassalehoon; wa a'oozo beka mimmasta'za minho 'ibadokal mukhlasoon."

In first Rakaat, the Qunoot is recited five times along with Takbirs (Allaho Akbar). Then after Ruku and Sajdah, the second Rakaat begins. In the second Rakaat Sura Shams is recited after Sura Hamd.

In Surah Shams (91st Sura) Allah has directed man to keep himself pure and to protect himself from sins. After the recitation of this Sura, the Qunoot is again recited but now only four times. Thereafter Ruku, Sajdah, Tashahhud and Salam are done in the usual way.

LESSON 52
PRAYER OF JAMA'AT

Prayer is offered individually and also in Jama'at (congregation). But there is great reward when it is offered in Jama'at.

Prayer in congregation gives us both worldly and spiritual benefits:

1. Islamic equality:

In the congregation, rich and poor, high and low, all stand shoulder to shoulder. This destroys the haughtiness of the rich and creates self-respect in the poor. The best scene of mankind's equality comes before us in congregational Prayer.

2. Unity:

In the congregational prayer, all have one intention, one language and identical actions. All kneel together. All prostrate together. This teaches us the lesson of the unity of the Muslims.

3. Love and Cooperation:

People meet with one another in the congregation. They know the problems and worries of each other and try to help each other. New things are known. Mutual love develops. Circle of friendship is widened. We get an opportunity to perfect our life in the light of others' experiences.

4. Discipline:

While offering prayer in Jama'at we stand in rows, follow the Imam of Jama'at and practice obedience to Command. This instills in us the discipline which is the essential feature of a community's life.

5. Prestige of Islam:

Our mosques remain thriving--due to prayer in Jama'at. It enhances the prestige of the Muslims, and the unity of the Muslims overawes the enemies of Islam.

6. Limitless Reward:

Allah has put a big reward for congregational prayers:

Our Holy Prophet (S.A.W.) and the Imams (A.S.) have laid great stress on congregational prayer.

The Holy Prophet (S.A.W.) said that if there are only 2 persons (Imam and only one Mamum) in Jama'at prayer, every Rakaat gets the reward of 150 prayers. The reward is increased by the increase in the number of persons. Thus, in a Jama'at prayer of 3 persons, every Rakaat gets reward of 600 prayers.

If there are 4, every Rakaat gets reward of 1,200 prayers.
If there are 5, every Rakaat gets reward of 2,400 prayers.
If there are 6, every Rakaat gets reward of 4,800 prayers.
If there are 7, every Rakaat gets reward of 9,600 prayers.
If there are 8, every Rakaat gets reward of 19,200 prayers.
If there are 9, every Rakaat gets reward of 38,400 prayers.
If there are 10, every Rakaat gets reward of 76,800 prayers.
If there are more than 10, then nobody can estimate its reward except Allah.

Your Lord has decreed:
You shall not serve any but Him,
And that you be kind to parents.
--Al-Isra: 23

LESSON 53
PRAYER OF MAYYIT (FUNERAL PRAYER)

Funeral prayer is Wajib-e-Kifai, i.e., it is obligatory on every Muslim but as soon as it is performed correctly by one of them, it does not remain obligatory on others; but if no one offers the prayer, everyone is a sinner. If the deceased was six years old, Prayer of Mayyit is Wajib. In offering this prayer, Taharat of the body or dress is not necessay; also Ghusl, Wudu (Wuzu) or Tayammum is not Wajib. But making intention of prayer (Niyyat) and facing Qibla are essential. The dead body should be placed in such a way that the head remains on the right of those who offer the prayer. In the case of the dead body of a male, the Imam should stand near his waist; and in the case of a female, near the chest.

Prayer of Mayyit has 5 Takbirs (including Takbiratul-Ihram). After first Takbir (i.e., Takbiratul Ihram) Kalema-e-Shahadat is recited. After 2nd Takbir, Salawat is recited. After 3rd Takbir, prayer is offered for all the Believers and Muslims. After 4th Takbir, prayer is offered especially for the deceased one. Then 5th Takbir is said and the prayer comes to an end.

The shortest method of offering this prayer is as follows:
Niyyat: I pray Salat-e-Mayyit of this corpse Wajib Qurbatan Ilallah.
Allaho Akbar.
Ashhado Al-la Ilaha Ilallaho Wahdahuu La Sharika Lah; Wa Ashhado Anna Mohammadan Abduhuu wa Rasuluh;
Allaho Akbar;
Allahumma Sally Ala Muhammadin wa Aale Muhammad;
Allaho Akbar;
Allahummaghfir lil Mumeneena wal Mumenaat;
Allaho Akbar;
Allahummaghfir Le Haazal Mayyit (In case the deceased is a female, say Allahummaghfir Le Haazehil Mayyit);
Allaho Akbar;
After the completion of the prayer, recite: "Rabbana Aaetena Fid-Dunya Hasanatan wa fil Aakhirati Hasanatan Wa qina Azaban-Naar."

It is necessary to mention that even if this prayer is offered by Jamaat, everyone has to recite the whole prayer. It is not correct just to say 'Allaho Akbar' and remain silent between the Takbirs. Such a prayer is invalid.

LESSON 54
SOM (Fasting)

SOM:

Som means to abstain from those things which break the fast, from Sub-he-Sadiq (true dawn) to Maghrib-time (sunset), in obedience to the commandments of Allah.

WAJIB SOMS:

Six Soms are Wajib, viz.
1. Month of Ramadan (Ramazan)
2. Som of Kaffara becoming Wajib for various reasons.
3. Som of Qada (Qaza)
4. Ten days of 'badal-ul-hadi' in Hajj
5. Third day of Itikaf
6. Som which becomes Wajib on account of Nazr, 'Ahad or Qasam (oath)

THE DOME OF ROCK, (Jerusalem) (Beit-ul-Muqqaddas).

CONDITIONS OF SOM:
Following are the conditions for the validity of Som:
1. Adulthood
2. Sanity
3. Not fainting
4. Remaining free from Haid (Haiz) and Nifas for whole day
5. Not being in danger of illness by keeping fast
5. Not remaining a 'Musafir' at the time of Zawal

LESSON 55
MUFTIRAT (The Things Which Break the Fast)

The things or actions which make a fast void (batil) are 9 in number:
1. Eating or drinking anything. 2. Sexual relations. 3. Doing any such thing by which semen comes out. 4. Speaking, writing or conveying by sign, any lie about Allah, Prophets, (S.A.W.); Imams (A.S.); or Bibi Fatima (S.A.). 5. Allowing thick dust, smoke, or steam to reach the throat. 6. Submerging the head in water. 7. Remaining in the condition of Janabat, Haid (Haiz) or Nifas up to Sub-he-Sadiq. 8. Enema with liquid. 9. Vomiting.

NOTE 1. All these things break the fast if they are committed intentionally. If a person forgets that he or she is fasting, and eats or drinks, his or her fast is correct. Likewise, if he or she vomits involuntarily, or speaks something about God or Imams (A.S.) which he or she thinks is correct (though in fact, it is wrong), or somebody else pushes him or her into water and his or her head goes into water or he or she sees dust coming toward him or her and tries his or her best to protect himself/herself from it, but still inhales some of it involuntarily, his or her fast is correct.

NOTE 2: Remaining in the condition of Janabat makes fast Batil in the month of Ramadan and in its Qada only. Other fasts are not affected by it.

NOTE 3: Not performing Ghusl (or Tayammum, if allowed) of Haid, or Nifas before Subh-e-Sadiq (true dawn) makes the fast Batil in the month of Ramadan only. Other fasts (including the Qada of Ramadan) are not affected by it.

NOTE 4: When a fast is broken by any of the above-mentioned Muftirat, or when a person does not fast (without any excuse, i.e., illness or travel), he or she has to pay Kafara, in addition to its Qada (Qaza).

KAFFARA
The Kaffara of breaking the fast of one day of Ramadan is:
1. Emancipating a slave;
2. If that is not possible, then fasting for two months consecutively;
3. And if that is also not possible, then feeding 60 poor Momins.

67

The Kaffara of breaking the Qada of one day of Ramadan, if broken after Zawal, is: 1. Feeding 10 poor Momins; 2. and if that is not possible, then fasting three days.

The Kaffara of breaking the fast of specified Nazar is:
1. Emancipating a slave;
2. If that is not possible, then feeding 10 poor Momins;
3. Or clothing 10 poor Momins;
4. And if one cannot do any of these, then fasting three days.

NOTE 1: In feeding, it is enough to give each man 1 1/2 pounds wheat or rice.

NOTE 2: Whenever in a Kaffara a certain thing is prescribed, its price is not acceptable. For instance, it is not allowed to give the price of 1 pound wheat, or the price of shirt and trousers to a poor man. It is obligatory to give him the grain or cloth.

NOTE 3: When a fast is broken by any Haram thing, like wine etc., all 3 Kaffaras are to be paid (emancipation of slave, 60 days fast, feeding 60 poor Momins), as a penalty.

NOTE 4: In two months' fast, at least 31 days should be fasted consecutively, The remaining 29 days may be fasted with gaps.

If a Musafir returns to his or her hometown or reaches a place where he or she intends to stay 10 days, before Zawal, and has not done anything which breaks the fast, he or she must do Niyyat to fast, and the fast will be valid. Likewise, if he or she begins journey after Zawal, then the fast of that day will remain valid.

If a person is afraid that by fasting his or her illness will increase, or he or she will become sick by fasting, or that the treatment of his or her disease will become difficult, he or she must break the fast. If he or she does keep fast, it would be null and void, and he or she, in addition, would be commiting a sin.

Being 'Baligh'* is not a condition of validity of fast; if a child keeps fast, it would be all right. But fast is not Wajib on a 'minor' (Ghair-Baligh).

* A boy becomes Baligh when he completes his 15th year. A girl becomes Baligh when she completes her 9th year.

Persons Exempted from Som (fasting):

The following persons are exempted from Som:
1.& 2. Old men and women, when due to their old age and weakness
   (a) it is not possible for them to fast, or
   (b) it is very difficult for them to fast.

3. A person who has a disease in which he or she remains ever-thirsty and
   (a) it is not possible, or
   (b) is very difficult for him or her to fast
4. A pregnant woman who is afraid
   (a) about her own health or
   (b) the health of the unborn child.
5. A mother who breast-feeds a baby (her own or another woman's) and is afraid that the fast
   (a) would endanger her health or
   (b) the health of the baby.

All persons listed in item 1 through 5 above are exempted from fasting on the following conditions:
1. In case of (b), they will have to pay Kaffara (penalty) approximately 1.5 pound (3/4 kilogram) wheat, rice or any such staple food, per day to a poor Shia Ithna Ashri. It is 'Ahwat' (recommended) to pay 1.5 kilogram of such food per day.
2. In cases of (a), they are not required to pay any Kaffara; but it is highly recommended.
3. The thirsty person will have to fast in Qada, if he or she is able to do so afterwards.
4. Pregnant women, or a nursing mother will have to fast in Qada after delivery or after weaning the child, as the case may be.
5. An old man and woman are not required (though recommended) to fast in Qada if he or she regains his or her strength.

LESSON 56
NAZR

Nazr is a vow, a voluntary undertaking, of an act of virtue, as binding one's self in gratitude for some special favor prayed for. It is a solemn promise to Allah.

Types of Nazr:
1. Nazr-e-Birr. It is called Nazrul-Mujazat (Shukr=Thanks). If a particular wish is fulfilled, then to undertake to do an act of virtue.
2. Nazr-e-Istidfa le-Balliyyah--for removal of a hardship or difficulty.
3. Nazr-e-Zajr--Nazr for reprimanding oneself on committing a sin, e.g., if I backbite someone, then I shall be bound to pray two rakaats prayer.

69

4. Nazr-e-Tabarru is a Nazr without any of the above conditions; e.g., to bind oneself to pray Tahajjud prayers during the month of Ramadan, for the sake of Allah.

Conditions of Nazr:
Nazr should be performed in the following manner:
1. A Nazr should be kept for the sake of Allah. It is essential to say "LILLAHI ALAIYYA" (It is, for Allah, upon me to do so) whilst doing Nazr.
2. A person doing Nazr must be adult and sane; and should do Nazr with his own free-will.
3. If an extravagant person, or one who is prevented by Shariat to deal in his property or wealth does any Nazr involving money or wealth, it is not valid.
4. If a husband asks his wife not to keep Nazr and whilst performing Nazr the rights of the husband are likely to be encroached upon, then the wife cannot possibly keep such a Nazr. However, if the husband has granted his permission, then he cannot stop his wife from performing the Nazr.
5. Whilst doing Niyyat of a Nazr one should be capable to perform the said Nazr. Otherwise the Nazr is void. For example, if one does a Nazr that he will go to Karbala on foot, and it is not possible, then such a Nazr is void.
6. A Nazr cannot be kept to give up "WAJIBAT" or "MUSTAHABBAT" or to carry out MAKROOH or HARAM because such a Nazr is void.
7. A Nazr should always be performed according to the original intention. For instance, if one keeps a Nazr to give charity or recite prayers on a particular day, then it should be performed on that very particular day and it should not be postponed to any other day.
8. If a person keeps a Nazr to fast on a particular day and he intentionally does not fast on that day, then he shall have to keep Qada (Qaza) and at the same time pay Kaffara. However, if he is prevented from fasting on that particular day because of a genuine reason, e.g., if he falls sick or travels for Hajj, then he shall have to keep Qada (Qaza) only; there is no Kaffara on him.
9. If one keeps a Nazr for the tomb (Rauda) of an Imam (A.S.) or a Martyr or any other pious person, then it is Ihtiyat-e-wajib to use it in its construction, light, etc.
10. If the Nazr is kept for an Imam (A.S.) or Martyr or any Imamzada, (e.g., if my patient becomes well, then I will give as Nazr, for the sake of Allah, $100, to Imam Husain, (A.S.), then if he had a "Niyyat" to use that

money in a particular purpose e.g. construction of Imambara), then it must be used for that purpose.

And if at the time of making Niyyat for that Nazr, he did not specify a particular use, then it is called "Nazr-e-Mutlaq" (unspecified Nazr); and in this case the money should be used in a purpose which has some connection with that Imam (A.S.) or Martyr. For example, for his needy Zawwar, or construction of his tomb, etc.

11. The money of 'Nazr-e-Mutlaq' may also be used for the purpose of spreading and/or strengthening the religion, and for the help of poor Shias.

12. When one wants to spend the money of Nazr (mentioned in Nos. 10 and 11), it is better to do Niyyat that one is using it on behalf of the Imam (A.S.) or Martyr concerned and that the reward is for that Imam (A.S.) or Martyr.

NOTE: Niyyat means intention; Nazr means promise, voluntary undertaking on self.

HERE IS THE TOMB OF FATIMA (S.A.), THE DAUGHTER OF THE APOSTLE OF GOD AND THE QUEEN OF THE WOMEN OF THE WORLD; HERE ALSO IS THE TOMB OF HASSAN IBNE ALI IBNE ABI TALIB (A.S.). HERE ALSO IS THE TOMB OF ALI IBN AL-HUSSAIN (A.S.). HERE ALSO IS THE TOMB OF MUHAMMAD IBNE ALI AL BAQIR (A.S.). HERE ALSO IS THE TOMB OF JA'FAR IBNE-MUHAMMAD EL SADIQ (A.S.).

71

LESSON 57
THE DEEDS WHICH BRING BLESSINGS
OR HAPPINESS (MUSTAHABBAT)

Deeds Which Bring Blessings

1. To rise early in the morning.
2. To speak truth.
3. To recite Sura Qul Huwallah whilst entering or leaving one's house.
4. To pray five times with full devotion.
5. To recite Sura Yasin (Ch.36) and Sura Tabarakalladhi Bi Yadihil Mulk (Ch.67) after prayers.
6. To enter a mosque before Adhan (Azan).
7. To go out for earning livelihood in the morning.
8. To do good to one's relatives.
9. To keep the house clean.
10. To pray for a Momin in his absence.
11. To sprinkle rose water on one's face.
12. To wash both hands before and after meals.
13. To recite Quran and Du'a after prayers.
14. To recite Sura Waqi'ah (Ch.56) after Isha prayers.
15. To be always in a state of Taharat (purity and cleanliness).
16. To help Momineen and fulfil their needs.
17. To wear ring of Aqeeq, Firoza and Yaqut (Agate, Turquoise and Ruby)
18. To recite supplications regularly for remission of sins seeking forgiveness of Allah.
19. To avoid appropriating unlawful money.
20. To light up the lamp before sunset.
21. To repeat Adhan when the Mu'adhin (Mo'azzin) announces it.
22. To thank Allah incessantly.
23. To pick up crumbs of food from the table cloth and eat them.
24. To sleep at night with Wudu (Wuzu)
25. To recite Adhan and Iqamah before Wajib Salat.

DEEDS WHICH BRING UNHAPPINESS
(MAKROOHAT)

1. To sleep until sunrise, after morning prayer.
2. To talk about worldly matters when Adhan is being recited.
3. To comb hair while standing.
4. To take false oath.
5. To be greedy.
6. To set foot on scraps of bamboo pen.
7. To eat in the state of Janabat.
8. To offer Salat hastily.
9. To sweep floor at night.
10. To pass urine while standing.
11. To consider a grain of food as worthless.
12. To perform Wudu in privy or latrine.
13. To neglect beggars.
14. To pass through a flock of sheep or herd of animals.
15. To put out a candle with puff of mouth.
16. To sit on a grave.
17. To bite one's nails.
18. To keep spider's web in the house.
19. To wipe the face with shirt sleeve or tail of dress.
20. To pass urine or to cleanse teeth in bathroom.
21. To sleep between Maghrib and Isha prayers.
22. To keep rubbish, filth etc., in the house.
23. To wash hands with clay.
24. To burn peel of onion or garlic.
25. To sit on the threshold
26. To wear black shoes.

****

QUESTIONS

Lessons 2/3

1. State whether the following were Imam, Panjatan or both:
(a) Hadret Hassan al Mujtaba. (b) Hadret Ali al Murtaza (c) Hadret Musa al Kazim.
2. Name the Imam whose life was shortest and the one whose life is the longest.

Lessons 4/7

1. Name the Books which were revealed to the Ulul-Azm Prophets.
2. Name the month of Fasting, the ninth month of Islamic Calendar.

Lessons 8/13

1. Prove in your own words the existence of God.
2. Give one Ayat to prove the oneness of Allah.
3. Why Qiyamat is necessary? When will it come?
4. Name the Imam with whom you will be called on the Day of Judgment?

Lessons 14/16

1. At what age a boy and a girl have to fulfill religious obligations?
2. Name the month in which Hajj is performed.
3. What will be the amount of Zakat paid by a man who has kept 200 silver coins?
4. How much Khums should be paid on a saving of Dollars one hundred and fifty?
   How shall this money be distributed?
5. When is Jehad wajib? Would you call it Jehad if people without the permission of Imam attack a country for worldly gains?
6. What do you understand by Amr-Bil-Maroof and Nahy-Anil-Munkar?
7. With whom is Tabarra done?
8. What is the meaning of Aalam?

Lesson 17

1. Give five examples of each of the following:
   WAJIB - HARAM - MAKROOH
2. Explain in brief the difference between Mushrik and Munafique.

Lesson 18
1. Give a single term:
   (a) for a thing taken illegally.
   (b) for a thing taken lawfully.
2. What is the difference between Muwalat and Tartib? Explain giving examples.

Lesson 19
1. Explain, with reason, whether the following things are Najis or Pak:
   (a) Urine of human being.
   (b) Dung of cow.
   (c) Stool of snake.
   (d) Hair of a dead man.
   (e) Dead body of a Muslim when it is still warm.
   (f) Sweat of a person lawfully Mujnib.

Lesson 20
Describe what is the effect of the following, giving reason for your answer:
1. A dog drinks from water which was exactly a Kur.
2. Najasat is mixed with rose-water more than a Kur.
3. A few drops of urine mixed with water more than a Kur.
4. A car splashes water on your clothes while it is heavily raining.
5. A pig licks a pot.
6. You walk barefoot on wet earth with najasat on your sole.
7. A najasat is dried by mere heat on an immovable thing.
8. A dead dog changes into earth.
9. You kill a mosquito which leaves blood on your hand.
10. A kafir accepts Islam.

Lesson 21
1. When wine and its container become clean?
2. Explain what is Istibra.
3. While visiting a Muslim (who deliberately ignores laws of Shariat you noticed a chair being najis. On your next visit, you happen to sit on the same chair with your wet clothes on. Are your clothes Pak or Najis?

Lesson 22
1. What is the method of Taharat after urinating?
2. With which things can Taharat be done after relieving bowels?
3. What are the conditions for Taharat with paper, etc.?

Lesson 23
1. Which are wajib actions in Wudu (Wuzu)?
2. Describe the Sunnats of Wudu (Wuzu).

Lesson 24
Explain briefly the effect of the following actions:
1. A man performed Wudu at a place where a signboard says: "No admission without permission."
2. A man performed Wudu at a public park.
3. You helped your friend in performing Wudu by pouring water on his hand.
4. A silver pot is used for performing Wudu.
5. You completed Wudu but it did not cleanse the sole of your foot which was najis.
6. A girl performs Wudu while her nails are covered with nail polish.
7. A girl performs Wudu while having hina color on her palms.
8. You poured water on hand starting from fingers going toward the elbow.

Lesson 25
When do the following Salat become wajib?
1. Salat-e-Ayaat.
2. Salat-e-Ijara.
3. Salat-e-Mayyit.
4. Salat-e-Juma.

Lesson 26
1. A man takes one minute for one Rakaat. The time is 6:26 p.m. The sun is to set at 6:30 p.m. and he has not prayed Zuhr and Asr yet. Which Salat should he pray first and why?
2. A man prays 'Isha at 6:15 p.m. which is the exact starting time of Maghrib? Is his 'Isha prayer valid? Why?
3. Differentiate between Fazilat time and reserve time.

Lesson 27
1. How will you find out the direction of Qibla in a Muslim village?
2. How should a man pray when he is uncertain of direction of Qibla?
3. In what direction should a man face while in toilet?

Lesson 28

Describe the effects of following actions, giving the reason for your answers:

1.(a) A Salat is performed in Tahir Ghasbi clothes.
  (b) A hair of a cat is on the cloth of a Mussali.
  (c) A belt made from a lawfully slaughtered cow is worn during prayer.
  (d) A woman is wearing a golden ring during her prayers.
  (e) A man has a handkerchief of pure silk in a pocket during the prayers.
  (f) A man while praying is wearing a cloth which has a few drops of blood of a Kafir on it.
  (g) A man prays in a dry najis place, but the place of Sajdah is Tahir.

2. Under what circumstances can a person pray without having clothes on?

Lesson 29

1. What is the reward of a prayer in Masjidul Haram?
2. What is the reward of a prayer in Masjid Jame?

Lesson 30

1. Are Adhan and Iqamah wajib?
2. Is "Ash-hadu An-na Ameeral Mo'ameneena Aliy-yan Hujatul-Lahh" a part of Adhan or Iqamah?

Lesson 31/38

1. Are the following things wajib-e-rukni, wajib-e-ghair-rukni or sunnat?
   RUKU - MUWALAAT - DHIKR-E-SAJDAH - SALAWAT after DHIKR - E - RUKU - TASHAHHUD - NIYYAT - QIYAM at the time of TAKBIRATUL IHRAM - SALAM - SAMI ALLAHU LIMAN HAMIDAH - QUNOOT - QIRAAT - TARTIB.
2. What will be the effect of the following:
   (a) You intentionally did not recite Qunoot in Salat.
   (b) In addition to the seven parts of your body, you also kept your nose on the earth during Sajdah.
   (c) You forgot Takbiratul-Ihram after Niyyat.
   (d) You left out one Sajdah in Salat by mistake.
   (e) While reciting Sura Al-Hamd you purposely kept your body moving.
3. What is the difference between 'Wajib-e-Rukni' and 'Wajib-e-Ghair Rukni'?

77

Lesson 39

Decribe the actions which invalidate a prayer.

Lesson 40/41

What are you supposed to do in the following:
1. Doubt occurred in Ruku as to whether you had recited Sura-e-Al-Hamd.
2. In Maghrib prayer a doubt occurred whether it was the 2nd or the 3rd Rakaat.
3. You became doubtful in a four Rakaat-prayer, at the time of Tashahhud whether you had prayed 1st Rakaat.
4. At the time of Maghrib you became doubtful whether you had prayed your 'Asr prayer properly.
5. You became doubtful in a four-Rakaat prayer before second Sajdah whether it was 2nd or 3rd Rakaat.

Lesson 42

State the remedial procedure for the following doubts:
1. In a four-Rakaat prayer doubt occurred whether it was the 3rd or the 4th Rakaat.
2. A doubt occurred after both Sajdah whether it was 2nd, 3rd or 4th Rakaat.
3. Doubt occurred after two Sajdahs whether it was the 2nd or the 4th Rakaat.
4. Doubt occurred while in Qiyam whether it was 5th or 6th Rakaat.

Lesson 43
1. Explain with examples when Sajdah-e-Sahv is wajib?
2. When does Salat-e-Ehtiyat become wajib?
3. How Sajdah-e-Sahv is done?

Lesson 44/45
1. Explain the difference between Ghusl-e-Tartibi and Ghusl-e-Irtimasi.
2. Which are wajib ghusls for a man?
3. Can a Junub person enter Imambargah to hear Majlis?
4. Can a Junub person recite Quran from memory?

Lesson 46
1. What is the minumum period of Haid and Nifas? What is the maximum duration?

2. Which things are Haram during the period of Haid and Nifas?
3. Can Haid start before the age of 9 years?

Lesson 47
1. What is Istihada?
2. Explain the difference between Istihada Mutawassita and Kathira.
3. What should be done in Istihada Qalila?

Lesson 48
1. (a) At noon, you have no water; but there is possibility of getting water long before sunset. Are you allowed to do Tayammum and pray Zuhr at noon?

(b) A person has been advised not to use cold water in any circumstances for doing either Wudu or Ghusl. Should he do Tayammum for prayers.?

(c) Water is sufficient for Wudu only if your horse or cow is denied water. Should you use that water for Wudu?

2. Name the things on which Tayammum is allowed.

Lesson 49
1. When prayer of Ayaat is Wajib?
2. What is the method of prayer of Ayaat?

LESSON 50
1. What is the meaning of Wajib-e-Takhyiri?
2. What are the conditions for Friday prayer?

Lesson 51
1. Is Eidain prayer Wajib now-a-days?
2. What is the method of Eidain prayer?

Lesson 52
1. Explain some social benefits of Jamaat prayer.
2. Give some spiritual benefits of Jamaat prayer.

Lesson 53
1. What is the meaning of "Wajib-e-Kifai?"
2. What is the method of Salat-e-Mayyit?
3. Is Wudu or Ghusl wajib for Salat-e-Mayyit?

Lesson 54
1. What are the conditions of validity of fasting?
2. Who are the persons exempted from fasting?

Lesson 55
1. Explain the result of the following actions on Fast:
(a) A person gets into water up to his chest.
(b) Forgetting that he was fasting, he drank water.
(c) Intentionally not doing Ghusl-e-Janabat up to Subhe-Sadik.
2. What is Kaffara for an aged person who cannot fast?

God and His Angels send blessings on the Prophet;
O ye that believe! send your blessings on him,
and salute him with all respect.
(Qur'an 33:56)

Refered on Lesson 5, page 13

Allah has sent in all 124,000 Prophets, all of whom were sinless. Many Prophets have been mentioned in the Holy Qur'an and in the Bible.
The following are some of the Prophets mentioned in the Holy Qur'an:

1. Adam	14. Dawud
2. Noah	15. Sulayman
3. Ibrahim	16. Dhul-Kifl
4. Ismael	17. Idriss
5. Isaac	18. Elias
6. Jacob	19. Zakariya
7. Yusuf	20. Yahya
8. Al-Yasa	21. Ayub
9. Yunus	22. Musa
10. Lut	23. Harun
11. Saleh	24. Isa
12. Hud	25. Muhammad
13. Shu'aib	

MAKKA, The Center of the World

The map below made on the principle of Mercator's projection gives a vivid picture of the situation of Makka in the center of the world.

In the Holy Quran, Ch. 52, Verse 7, Makka is described as "THE MOTHER CITY" (UMM-AL-QURA) because it is destined to be the spiritual center of the world. Already after the passage of 1400 years since its advent, Islam is the most widespread religion of all the religions in the world.

The arrows in the map show the direction in which the Muslims all over the world face the Kaaba at Makka when saying their daily prayers. The Kaaba is also the birthplace of Hazrat Ali Alaihis Salaam.

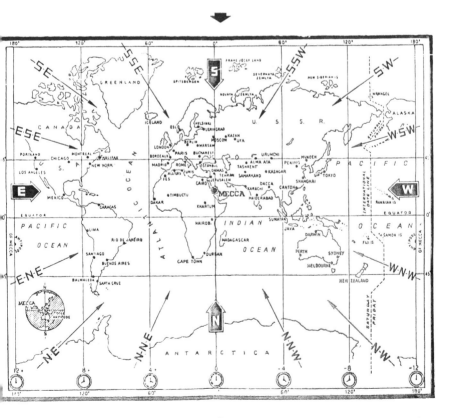